THE BOOK
OF
GREAT
QUOTES

THE BOOK OF GREAT QUOTES

COMPILED AND INTRODUCED BY
FLAMUR VEHAPI

CLARITAS
BOOKS

2 3 4 5 6 7 8 9 10

CLARITAS BOOKS

Bernard Street, Swansea, United Kingdom
Milpitas, California, United States

CLARITAS
BOOKS

First Edition: December 2018
Second Edition: May 2022

Typeset in Minion Pro 14/11

The Book of Great Quotes
Compiled and introduced by Flamur Vehapi

A CIP catalogue record for this book is available from the British Library

ISBN 978-1-905837-64-9

FOR MY BELOVED
SON, SUHAIL

Flamur Vehapi is a researcher, poet, literary translator, academic and a leadership and success coach. He received his A.A. and B.S. in psychology with a minor in history, and in 2013, he received his M.A. from Portland State University in Conflict Resolution. Currently, he is a PhD candidate at Pacific University for Education and Leadership. Flamur taught social sciences at Rogue Community College and Southern Oregon University, and more recently he taught at various institutions in the Middle East. His works include *The Alchemy of Mind* and *A Cup with Rumi*, both collections of spiritual poems, and his most recent books are Peace and Conflict Resolution in Islam, and The Book of Albanian Sayings. Flamur and his family currently live in Oregon, USA.

Contents

APPENDICES

A Brief Timeline of the Early Caliphate[a]

610   Prophet Muhammad receives the first revelation of the Quran

622   The Hijrah takes place – Prophet Muhammad and his followers flee the Quraysh persecutions and migrate to Madinah; the Islamic calendar begins

628   The Treaty of Hudaybiyyah is signed by the Prophet and the Quraysh, and peace is established in the region between Muslims and non-Muslims

630   Makkans violate the peace treaty. In return the Prophet goes to capture Makkah and the city surrendered voluntarily; the Makkans are forgiven

632   Prophet Muhammad passes away; Abu Bakr as-Siddiq is chosen as his representative (i.e. caliph)

---

[a] See *Appendix B* for a detailed timeline of the history of Islam.

634 Abu Bakr passes away; Umar bin al-Khattab is put in charge by the Muslim leadership as the next caliph

638 Jerusalem is captured (the city is considered to be Islam's third holiest site after Makkah and Madinah)

644 Umar bin al-Khattab is assassinated; Uthman bin Affan becomes the next caliph

656 Uthman is assassinated and many, but not all, accept Ali ibn Abi Talib as the fourth caliph; later on two opposing camps of Muslims are formed

661 Ali is assassinated; Muawiyah I takes control of the caliphate and founds the Umayyad dynasty, moving his capital to Damascus

Introduction

Through the centuries, the world has come to know some great leaders as shapers and makers of civilisations. Many of them are recognised and honoured to this day, others have been forgotten, and some for one reason or another have often been deliberately ignored in western writings. The wise leaders discussed and quoted in the following pages are unfortunately from the last category. Although these exceptional personalities did not build palaces or compose volumes of books, they left behind a legacy that is unmatched in human history. Inspired by the message of their teacher, Prophet Muhammad, to this day they continue to touch hearts and inspire lives throughout the globe. These great polymaths are known as the first four caliphs of Islam, which include Abu Bakr as-Siddiq ﷺ, Umar bin al-Khattab ﷺ, Uthman bin Affan ﷺ and Ali ibn Abi Talib ﷺ

The caliphs explored here, and many others that followed them, were remarkable figures in every sense of the word. They embodied all characteristics of true leadership that we can think of today, and much more, which we will look at in this book. To start with, unlike many leaders around the world today, especially heads of state, the caliphs did not beg people for their votes or election, nor did they make the empty promises typical of modern politics. The caliphs were carefully selected and appointed by the council of elders and the heads of their communities, and *then* were given the pledge of allegiance by the people, men and women, young and old. In fact, unlike many leaders of our nations, the caliphs in point refused to take such positions of leadership, fearing that they would not be able to bear such a burden of responsibility or carry out such a task successfully, and asked that someone better than them be appointed for such a post. This was the first reaction of Abu Bakr, for example; however everyone in the community knew that there was no person on the face of the earth who could have been more experienced and qualified than Abu Bakr for the position of caliph.[1] After accepting the position, he humbly said, "If you find what I say and do to be true, then assist me, and if you find what I say and do to be false, then advise me and set me straight."[2] And how many of our leaders take into consideration the words of the people, or who would dare try and correct them?

This work is very brief and a modest one, and it's aim is to simply give the reader a glimpse of the lives and wisdom of these great personalities of Islam. Those interested in a more in-depth study of the lives and contributions of the Caliphs should check out the resources listed in the bibliography section of this book.

The Caliphs and
the Caliphate

A caliph, or *khalifah* in Arabic, is a successor of Prophet Muhammad and a spiritual leader of the Muslim community. This means that after the passing away of the Prophet, the leaders of the Muslim world were to be the successors of the Prophet.[3] The dominion of the caliph is called a Caliphate, a term greatly misused and abused today.[4]

There have been a number of caliphs throughout Islamic history, but the most commonly known are the Rightly- Guided Caliphs, also known as *al-khulafa al-rashideen*.[a] These outstanding personalities, close companions of the Prophet, include Abu Bakr as-Siddiq (r. 632-634), Umar bin al- Khattab (r. 634-644), Uthman bin Affan (r. 644-656), and the son-in-law of the Prophet, Ali ibn Abi Talib (r. 656-661). During the reign of these Rightly-Guided Caliphs, the Caliphate grew well beyond the known Arabian territories; all of this occurred within thirty years of their rule. After the assassination of Ali, however, and the civil war that came with it, the governor of

---

[a] Also known as the Rashidun Caliphs. See Appendix A for a list of caliphs and sultans.

Syria, Muawiyah ibn Sufyan, took over the Caliphate and gradually it turned into a family dynasty.[5]

The dynasty that originated with the rise of Muawiya I is known in history as the Umayyad dynasty. The dynasty reigned from 661 to 750 CE, and during this period the seat of the Muslim caliphate was moved from Madinah, where it had originally started with the Prophet, to Damascus in Syria. Even during this time, the new dynasty vastly expanded, including lands from Spain to western India. This progress, however, came at a price when it was challenged from within. As the Sunni-Shia split occurred, and sectarian tensions began to grow, many of the Shia rejected the authority and legitimacy of the Umayyads, and called for the descendants of Ali to rule the *ummah*. The great deal of trials and tribulations from within slowly brought down the dynasty.

Soon after the revolts in the Caliphate, the rebels declared their own dynasty, known as the Abbasid dynasty, named after Abbas ibn Abd al-Muttalib, the uncle of the Prophet. The new dynasty, like the Ummayyads, quickly rose to power, reigning from 750 to 1258 CE. The dynasty moved even farther away from traditional Arab lands and established its capital in the newly founded city of Baghdad, present-day Iraq. It was during this time, the Abbasid period, a millennium before the European Enlightenment, that the Muslim world experienced its own scientific revolution and age of enlightenment. Muslim students and scholars, with strong encouragement from the caliphs themselves, excelled in their achievements in fields like science, mathematics, astronomy, philosophy, medicine and many other realms of knowledge. Although not much credit is given to Muslims today, such great achievements and developments impact our lives to this day.[6] The early stages of the Caliphate were a driving force behind these new advancements and growth.

Abu Bakr as-Siddiq ﷺ

Abu Bakr's conviction and belief in Islam and his support for his closest friend, Muhammad, was so great that it earned him the title *as-Siddiq,* the upright (also translated as "truthfulness" and "true friend"). Later he was given the glad tidings of paradise by none other than the Prophet himself.[a] According to tradition, Abu Bakr was born in the year 573 CE in the ancient city of Makkah, present-day Saudi Arabia. Abu Bakr's family belonged to the clan of Bani Taym, a branch of the ruling tribe of Quraysh. His real name was Abdullah ibn Abi Quhafah, but as a child, like many children of his time, he developed a fondness for camels, so he was given the nickname of *Abu Bakr,* meaning the father of a camel's foal (nicknames are very common in the Arab culture to this day).[7]

Abu Bakr seems to have enjoyed a well-mannered upbringing, and like the rest of his noble family, he was widely respected even as a young man among his tribesman. As he grew older, he was widely admired for his exemplary and wholesome nature and as a result he later held high ranking positions within the leadership of the tribe. As the tradition holds, everyone spoke highly of him and loved him for his assistance of the poor, generosity, and his hospitality. Abu Bakr was also a very successful businessman. Because of his fairness in dealing with people, charitable giving, and also large investments and trade in the region, going as far as Syria and the surrounding areas, he quickly became one of the wealthiest people in Makkah.[8] He would later of course spend most of this wealth in the cause of Islam. After the passing

---

[a] In a hadith in Jami at-Tirmidhi, the Prophet specified by name that the following ten of his companions were guaranteed Paradise. He said "Abu Bakr is in Paradise, Umar is in Paradise, Uthman is in Paradise, Ali is in Paradise, Talhah is in Paradise, Az-Zubair is in Paradise, Abdur Rahman bin Awf is in Paradise, Sa'd bin Abi Waqqas is in Paradise, Sa'id ibn Zayd is in Paradise, and Abu Ubaidah bin Al-Jarrah is in Paradise."

away of the Prophet, in 632 CE, community leaders chose Abu
Bakr as the successor to the Prophet. As a leader, Abu Bakr
was remarkable, fair and humble. Sir William Muir (1819–
1905) described him as "simple, diligent, wise and impartial."[9]
His achievements as a caliph are too many to recount here, but
one of note was his compilation of the text of the Quran into
one complete book.[10] Abu Bakr's life came to an end in August
634 CE of old age, in his beloved city of Madinah. Shortly before his death, however, he urged the Muslim community to
accept Umar as his successor.[11]

Umar bin al-Khattab ﷺ

The second caliph of Islam, Umar bin al-Khattab, was born in
586 CE, also in Makkah. Umar came from the clan of
Adiy of the Makkan tribe of Quraysh. Like most of his
tribesmen, Umar originally opposed Prophet Muhammad and
his message of Islam, and went as far as wanting to take the
Prophet's life in order to preserve the old ways of his tribe. Having come in direct contact with the new message around 615
CE, however, Umar then accepted Islam and, like Abu Bakr, became one of the staunchest supporters of the Prophet and his
message. Having enjoyed such a great status in the company of
the Prophet himself, Umar also served as the Prophet's chief adviser, and was by his side until the final days of the Messenger of
God. Moreover, because of his uncompromising justice and
fairness, Umar was also referred to as *al-Faruq*, the discerner
between truth and falsehood. He was also the first of the caliphs
to be given the title "Commander of the Faithful."[12]

The wise person that he was, Umar played a great role in
encouraging the community to accept Abu Bakr as their caliph. For the time of his reign (632 – 634 CE), Abu Bakr relied
heavily on Umar for support and advice in matters of religion
and state; analogously, Umar also depended on Abu Bakr, who

was his senior both in age and in Islam.[13] On his deathbed, it was Abu Bakr himself who appointed Umar to take his place as the next caliph. Such a decision, of course, was unanimously approved by the Muslim council at the time.

As a caliph, the 'Commander of the Faithful' completely transformed the Arabian-based Muslim state. Under his reign, the new Muslim empire not only expanded quickly and vastly, it also developed remarkable administrative and legal principles to rule such ample lands and diverse communities; a challenge never before faced by any Arab leader at the time. Umar himself was widely respected for his just rule and devotion to his faith, as well as the well-being of his community and the *ummah* at large. Ten years into his reign, however, in 644 CE Umar was treacherously assassinated. He was buried next to his beloved Prophet and Abu Bakr as- Siddiq in his treasured city of Madinah (his desire had been to die there as a martyr).[14]

Uthman bin Affan ﷺ

The son of a wealthy merchant from the powerful Banu Umayya clan of the tribe of Quraysh, Uthman was born in 576 CE in the city of Taif, present-day Saudi Arabia.[a] Although his clan had opposed the message and the Prophet Muhammad with great hostility, after a brief discussion with Abu Bakr, Uthman requested to be sent to the house of the Prophet where he accepted Islam on the spot. As a convert to the new faith, Uthman was a force to be reckoned with; he benefited the new community tremendously with his deep wisdom and his wealth. Being a close companion of the Prophet, later Uthman had also served as an adviser to both Abu Bakr and Umar. Uthman was a scribe of the Quran, and one who had memorised the noble book cover to cover.[15]

---

[a] There are accounts that Uthman was born in 577 CE instead, however the exact year remains unknown.

It was after the assassination of Umar that the Muslim council was faced with the question whether Uthman or Ali was to succeed the late caliph. Since Uthman was Ali's senior by over two decades, the selection committee naturally chose Uthman as the *ummah's* third caliph. Ali, of course, the wise person that he was, even after this decision was always by Uthman's side as an adviser and a close friend.

During the reign of Uthman, the empire witnessed not only a phase of continued expansion and development, but also great economic prosperity. Uthman not only improved the welfare of the people, he also raised people's fixed allowances put in place by his predecessors. The caliph himself, however, with all the wealth in the public treasury, never took a salary for himself, as he was able to sustain himself and his family through his own resources as a successful businessman.

As civil strife began to spread in different parts of the caliphate, however, a group of outsider rebels, dissatisfied with the election of Uthman, successfully penetrated the caliph's house and assassinated him. Thus, the reign of Uthman ibn Affan ended in 656 CE. Undoubtedly, the death of Uthman was a great loss to the faithful.[16]

Ali ibn Abi Talib

The fourth of the Rightly-Guided Caliphs was Ali ibn Abi Talib, the cousin and later son-in-law of the Prophet Muhammad. Ali, the son of Abu Talib from the prominent tribe of Quraysh, was born in 600 CE in the sacred city of Makkah. Having been raised in the household of the Prophet himself, Ali was the first child to accept Islam. The young convert to the faith was by the Prophet's side from his childhood to the time of the Prophet's passing in 632.

Ali was an exceptionally devout person, wise beyond his years, and one of the bravest in the battlefield. Because of his many great personal qualities and commitment to Islam, he was known by names like the "lion of God," "father of dust," "the gate of knowledge," and so on. Ali had the special blessing of marrying the daughter of the Prophet, Fatimah al-Zahra, and it was their offspring who carried on the lineage of the Prophet Muhammad.[17] After the passing of the Prophet, Ali focused mainly on his devotion to God and serving his family, although he was also a trusted adviser to all the caliphs discussed previously. When the assassination of Uthman took place, however, the Muslim council chose Ali as the fourth caliph of Islam. Ali reigned from 656 to 661 CE, ruling a vast empire. Unfortunately, during his reign he also witnessed a great deal of turmoil and civil unrest. In 661, a group of the Kawarij[18] rebels attacked Ali while he was performing his morning prayers at the Grand Mosque of Kufah. The civil unrest went on as Ali was leaving this world in the month of Ramadan, the holiest month in Islam. Ali died in the same year in the city of Kufah, present-day Iraq, and with this the great *Rashidun Caliphate* period came to an end.[19]

A Note from
the Editor

The process of collecting these sayings from such a vast body of literature was not an easy feat. The most challenging section in this book, however, was the collection and verification of the sayings of Ali ibn Abi Talib. Many of the quotes I found have been, intentionally or not, attributed to him. It seems that some think that by doing so, they will elevate the status of Ali, not realising that only a few in human history have reached Ali's level, status and grandeur. All of sayings in this collection have been carefully selected and cross-examined for authenticity and accuracy. A great number of reliable books, articles, websites, and apps have been consulted in order to accurately convey the meanings of these maxims. Many of them are found with different wording, and I have selected the most commonly used wording (often found online). Although tempting, those quotes with questionable sources and authenticity or found only in a few online sites have been left out.

As far as the introductory commentaries of this work are concerned, they are derived from the Quran commentaries, the vast hadith literature, as well as the referenced works found at the end of this book. The Quran translations are mainly from Abdel Haleem's *The Quran,* and Sahih International's *The Quran,* but other translations have also been consulted occasionally. As for the hadith literature utilised here, the most commonly cited works are the collections of Imam al-Bukhari and that of Imam Muslim, *Sahih al-Bukhari* and *Sahih Muslim* respectively. Other collections include *Sunan Abu Dawud, Sunan Ibn Majah, Jami at- Tirmidhi, Sunan Bayhaqi, ibn Kathir's al-Bidaya wal Nihaya,* and others as indicated in the footnotes, endnotes and bibliography.

On the Divine

Like Judaism and Christianity, Islam is a monotheistic faith, and as such, oneness of God is at the core of its teachings. In Islam, however, God "is unique and exalted above everything He creates, and His greatness cannot be compared to His creation...He is the only one deserving of any worship and the ultimate purpose of all creation is to submit to Him."[20] This concept is best described in the Quran itself:

Say, "He is God, [who is] One, God, the Eternal Refuge. He neither begets nor is born, Nor is there to Him any equivalent."[a]
In another verse the Creator revealed:

Indeed, I am God. There is no deity except Me, so worship Me and establish prayer for My remembrance.[b]

In these Quranic injunctions, and in many other cases, the All-Mighty describes Himself plainly to people without leaving any room for confusion or doubt; it clearly states that God

---

[a] Quran 112: 1-4.
[b] Quran 20:14.

(Allah)[a] is One and exalted over all things, the Everlasting, and only He[b] is all-capable, and as such only He deserves to be worshiped. Consequently, from an Islamic point of view,

Fully accepting the oneness of God is to accept that He is distinct from everything else. It would not suit God's majesty and glory to associate the limited attributes of His creation to Him because He is not restricted in any way, while His creation is. He is the First with no beginning and the Last with no end. Everything in the universe was created by His will. He is not confined by space or time and He is the only One who is in control and provides for His creation.[21] Furthermore, since the first days of Islam in Arabia, Muslims have stayed away from making any depictions of God, or ascribing any human attributes to Him, as people of some other faiths have done through the ages with their prophet and/or sages. Such acts are considered blasphemous in Islam since God is beyond what a human can imagine of Him. As a result, knowing that God's characteristics cannot be conceptualized by human reason, to this day Muslims speak of God, His nature and attributes only to the extent of what God has revealed about Himself in the Quran and what Prophet Muhammad has said about Him in the *hadith*. The Quran describes:

> *There is no god but He, the Living, the Everlasting. Slumber seizes Him not, nor sleep. To Him belongs all that is in the heavens and the earth. Who is there that shall intercede with Him save by His leave? He knows*

---

[a] Note here that even non-Muslim Arabic speakers refer to God as *Allah*, which clearly goes to show that, despite their theological differences, Muslims worship the same one Deity as Jews and Christians, among others.

[b] The pronoun *He* used here, and in other cases and forms, is a limitation of languages, like English, without a gender-neutral third-person singular pronoun. God ascribes to no gender since that is a humanly quality, therefore using gender-specific pronouns like *He* or *Him* to refer to the Divine is not technically correct, and such limitation is not the case with Arabic, the language of the Quran.

what lies before them, and what is after them, and they comprehend not anything of His knowledge save such as He wills. His throne comprises the heavens and earth. The preserving of them oppresses Him not; He is the All-High, the All-Glorious.[a] And this is how the caliphs discussed here seem to have approached the question of the Divine.[b]

He who has a taste for the love of God can have no taste for the love of the world.[22]
– **Abu Bakr as-Siddiq** ﷺ

Praise God, for through praise, His blessings multiply.[23]
– **Umar bin al-Khattab** ﷺ

Fear only God, for He alone lives; all other things are liable to perish.[24]
– **Umar bin al-Khattab** ﷺ

Mention what you will of the greatness of God, but God is greater than anything you say.[25]
– **Ali ibn Abi Talib** ﷺ

The word of God is the medicine of the heart.[26]
– **Ali ibn Abi Talib** ﷺ

---

[a] Quran 2:255.

[b] Although the word "fear" is used for *taqwah* here and in other instances, what it almost always implies is God-consciousness, piousness, virtue, being cognizant of God, among other things.

On Time and the
Life of this World

From an Islamic perspective, as is the case with some other belief systems, the life of this world is a transient one full of tests, while the real and everlasting life is that of the Afterlife. With regard to this, the Quran says:

> *Truly, the life of this world is nothing but a (quick passing) enjoyment, and verily, the Hereafter that is the home that will remain forever.*[a]

On this point Prophet Muhammad said, "What do I have to do with this life? Verily, my example in this life is the example of a traveler who went on a journey during a summer day, took shelter under a tree during a part of a day, then went on and left it." In another instance he advised, "Be in this world as though you were a stranger or a wayfarer."[b] However, being "as though you were a stranger or of wayfarer" in this world does

---

[a] Quran 40:39
[b] Hadith in *Sahih al-Bukhari.*

not necessarily mean that we are to renounce the world and everything in it, as some have interpreted this to mean; if that were the case, the Prophet himself and his honourable Companions would have been among the first to follow such a practice. In actuality, the Prophet was a man of both worlds; in addition to being a prophet of God, he was also a merchant and earned his living through hard work. Moreover, two of his closest Companions, Abu Bakr and Uthman, as a point in case, were two of the wealthiest men in their region at the time. These men, among hundreds of others, were certainly devout, and spent a great deal of their time in prayer and remembrance of God, but they also did physical work and earned their living through business dealings. In fact, the Prophet instructed the Muslims to often ask God for bounty and good in this world and in the Hereafter.[27]

What we learn from these righteous people is that, yes, they had money and wealth, but money was in their hands and not in their hearts, as seen from their constant giving to those in need. What all this means for us today is that one should certainly live this life to the fullest, within the bounds of what is permissible, but always keep in mind that this is not all there is to it, and that what we do here, in this world, we will find in the Hereafter, or as it has been said "what you have planted here, you will harvest there." Moreover, we have to continuously remember that this world is a temporary one, and that we are not to get attached to it. We are to live a balanced life where there is room for family, work and enjoyment, but at the same time we should always prioritise faith, and not lose focus in life. Nowadays, losing focus in life seems to be the case with many people because of all the distractions we face from all directions. These heedless individuals seem to be living life as if they are going to live in this world forever, but that is merely a self-deception. This life, like everything else, will come to an end, and there is nothing we can take with us to our graves except for our deeds. This is why a companion of the Prophet used to say,

"In the evening do not expect [to live until] the morning, and in the morning do not expect [to live until] the evening. Take [advantage of] your health before times of sickness, and [take advantage of] your life before your death."[28] Examining their words, actions and lifestyle, the caliphs mentioned here understood this concept clearly.

Our abode in this world is transitory; our life therein is but a loan. Our breaths are numbered, and our indolence is manifest.[29]
– **Abu Bakr as-Siddiq**

O man, you are busy working for the world, while the world is busy trying to turn you out.[30]
– **Abu Bakr as-Siddiq**

Have earnestness for death, and you will have life.[31]
– **Abu Bakr as-Siddiq**

This world is the marketplace of the faithful. Day and night are their capital; good deeds are their commodity; Paradise is their profit; and Hellfire is their loss.[32]
– **Abu Bakr as-Siddiq**

We were the lowliest of people, but God gave us might and glory through Islam. If we seek glory through other than what God gave us glory through,

He will abase us (again).[33]
– **Umar bin al-Khattab** ﷺ

I do not like this world except for three things: the place where my forehead touches the ground in prostration, the places where people gather for knowledge, seeking good words as they would choose the best dates from the dish, and striving in God's way.[34]
– **Umar bin al-Khattab** ﷺ

He who does not know evil will fall into it.[35]
– **Umar bin al-Khattab** ﷺ

The less of the world, the freer you live.[36]
– **Umar bin al-Khattab** ﷺ

I am surprised at three things: a) [A] man runs from death while death is inevitable b) One sees minor faults in others, yet overlooks his own major faults c) When there is any defect to one's cattle he tries to cure it, but does not cure his own defects.[37]
– **Umar bin al-Khattab** ﷺ

Four things are useless: a) Knowledge without practice b) Wealth without expenditure in the way of God c) Piety for the sake of show prompted by worldliness d) A long life with no stock of good deeds.[38]
– **Uthman bin Affan** ﷺ

Worrying about this world is a darkness in the heart, while worrying about the hereafter is a light in the heart.[39]
– **Uthman bin Affan** ﷺ

You are in a temporary world and there is only the
rest of your life. So, act good as much as you can for
if you live for today, you may die tomorrow. Since the
world is built on vanity, do not let it make you feel
self-conceit and do not let anything forget that God
loves not vanity. Get telling lessons from the experiences of others; then work hard. Do not forget this
for God does not forget you. Where are the sons of
the world and its brethren who built it and enjoyed it
for long? Didn't it spit them out? Throw the world
where God threw it. And beseech the afterworld for
God set an example for it.[40]
– Uthman ibn Affan ﷠

The greatest of all follies is to love the world.[41]
– Ali ibn Abi Talib ﷠

The likeness of this worldly life is that of a snake: soft
to the touch, it will kill you with its poison. So turn
away from what impresses you of it, since what stays
with you is so little. And do not be concerned about
it, since you are certain about its parting. And be
most happy in it when you are most heedful of it; for
every time its companion takes solace in one of its
delights, it gives way to one of its woes…[42]
– Ali ibn Abi Talib ﷠

The days of your life go by like clouds, so do good
while you are alive.[43]
– Ali ibn Abi Talib ﷠

Verily, this worldly life is departing and the hereafter
is approaching and each of them has its children. So

be children of the hereafter, not children of this world, for today there are (opportunities to do) deeds and there is no reckoning, but tomorrow there will be reckoning and no deeds.[44]
– **Ali ibn Abi Talib** ﷺ

Detachment is not that you should own nothing, but that nothing should own you.[45]
– **Ali ibn Abi Talib** ﷺ

Life consists of two days, one for you, one against you. So when it's for you, don't be proud or reckless, and when it's against you, be patient, for both days are a test for you.[46]
– **Ali ibn Abi Talib** ﷺ

People are asleep as long as they live; they are awakened when they die.[47]
– **Ali ibn Abi Talib** ﷺ

Every breath of man brings him nearer to death.[48]
– **Ali ibn Abi Talib** ﷺ

Everyone who is taken by death asks for more time, while everyone who still has time makes excuses for procrastination.[49]
– **Ali ibn Abi Talib** ﷺ

This world lasts for an hour: Spend it in obedience [of God].[50]
– **Ali ibn Abi Talib** ﷺ

On Self-Control
and Vain Desires

Self-control is unfortunately a virtue lacking in our societies to-day. Because of this, we often see people being driven by their desires and temptations in life, which in turn fuels their search for instant gratification. This cannot be a good thing for the human being itself and the society at large; it is in fact a destructive way of life. Regarding these people, the Quran says, *"...they only follow their own lusts. And who is more astray than one who follows his own lusts, without guidance from God..."*[a]

As far as Islam is concerned, self-control is a quality that is embedded in its system of beliefs, and as a result, it is also a cornerstone for each Muslim's way of life. Life as we know it is full of temptations, and Muslims are required to stay away from that which is forbidden by lowering their gaze, for instance, avoiding intoxicants, controlling their anger, thinking clearly before speaking, and so on. Moreover, the five pillars of Islam are all about patience and self-control. During the month of Ramadan, as a case in point, which can fall during cold weather or

---

[a] Quran 28:50.

extreme heat, Muslims around the world go without food and water from sunrise to sunset. This is an exercise of great self-control for young and old, and those who practice such self-restraint are promised great rewards in this life and the Hereafter. On this, the Quran says, "...*as for him who feared standing before his Lord, and restrained himself from impure evil desires and lusts. Verily, Paradise will be his abode.*"[a]

Various psychologists have conducted a number of studies and experiments on self-control in order to understand its long and short-term effects on human behaviour. One such experiment was the Stanford marshmallow experiment on delayed gratification. Here, A group of children aged 4-6 years old were each given a marshmallow. Each child was told that he or she could eat the marshmallow as soon as the experimenter left, i.e. straight away, or they could wait until the experimenter returned approximately 15 minutes later at which time they could have two marshmallows. Later when the children were revisited as adolescents it was found that those who delayed gratification scored higher in exams. They were described by their parents as having the ability to plan, handle stress, and concentrate without becoming distracted, and they exhibited self-control in difficult situations.[51] It is interesting to consider that when revisited in their 40s "those children who were unable to delay gratification in the marshmallow test performed poorly on self-control tasks."[52] On the other hand, those who waited longer for the rewards showed better life outcomes in general.[53] On this note, those who look into the life of the Prophet Muhammad, for example, quickly note that he was a man of tremendous self- control, from his childhood until his death. Moreover, the Prophet taught his followers to value and practice this virtue exactly the same way.

---

[a] Quran 79:40-41.

During his lifetime, the Prophet was constantly provoked by his enemies in order to elicit words unbecoming of him, and also was prodded to break a truce or fight, was offered money, women and power, but he declined all by choosing to practice self-control. He knew that this was more pleasing to his Creator than anything anyone else had to offer to him. In one instance, among many others, he is recorded to have said, "The strong person is not he who has physical strength but he that can control his anger."[a] Another time he said, "God fills with faith one who swallows his anger for God's sake."[b]

> If you want to control other people, first control yourself.[54]
> – **Abu Bakr as-Siddiq** 🌸

> Do not follow vain desires for verily he prospers who is preserved from lust, greed and anger.[55]
> – **Abu Bakr as-Siddiq** 🌸

> Do not become mad with love for anyone, nor seek to destroy with your dislike...[this] means that when you love anyone, there is the danger of falling head over heels, like a child, and when you dislike someone, you become bent upon destroying him.[c]
> – **Umar bin al-Khattab** 🌸

> For a servant of God, there is nothing sweeter than the swallowing of his own anger. Neither milk nor honey can be compared to it.[56]
> – **Umar bin al-Khattab** 🌸

[a] Hadith in *Sahih al-Bukhari* and *Sahih Muslim*.
[b] Hadith in *Musnad Ahmad*.
[c] Narration in *Adab al-Mufrad*.

Avoid alcohol, for it is the mother of all evils.[57]
– **Uthman bin Affan** ﷺ

Take best control of two things: your heart after a defeat, your head after a victory.[58]
– **Ali ibn Abi Talib** ﷺ

The tongue is like a lion. If you let it loose, it will wound someone.[59]
– **Ali ibn Abi Talib** ﷺ

Surely, silence can sometimes be the most eloquent reply.[60]
– **Ali ibn Abi Talib** ﷺ

The thing I fear for you most is following desires and having extensive hopes (about this worldly life). Following one's desires blocks you from the truth, and having extensive hopes makes you forget the hereafter.[61]
– **Ali ibn Abi Talib** ﷺ

The strongest amongst you is he who subdues his self.[62]
– **Ali ibn Abi Talib** ﷺ

Jealousy devours virtue as fire devours fuel.[63]
– **Ali ibn Abi Talib** ﷺ

Silence is the best reply to a fool.[64]
– **Ali ibn Abi Talib** ﷺ

Being deprived of something is better than being indebted to somebody.[65]
– **Ali ibn Abi Talib** ﷺ

On Truthfulness, Honesty and Intention

Yusuf Estes, an esteemed Muslim leader, once wrote, "Truthfulness is one of the pillars on which the moral survival of the world depends."[66] It is one of the greatest misfortunes of our time that many individuals today have completely pushed aside, and others have lost, the virtue of truthfulness, whether that is being truthful and honest with oneself or with others in their daily dealings. These people lie and cheat others every time they are presented with such an opportunity. We see this in our marketplaces, advertising campaigns, within various corporations, and even in the institutions that were created for the sole purpose of protecting and assisting their citizens. Although many countries nowadays are blessed with a great amount of resources and wealth, we see many of their citizens starving or living on streets, and unable to integrate into society due to the vicious cycle of structural violence and corruption in the system created and sustained by dishonest and deceptive leadership.

Islam has placed great emphasis on truthfulness, being honest in our daily lives, and having pure intentions whether it is concerning ourselves, others, or God. In the Quran the Creator says,

> O you who believe! Be mindful of God, and be with those who are true (in word and deeds).[a]

and in another verse:

> O you who have attained to faith! Remain conscious of God, and [always] speak with a will to bring out [only] what is just and true.[b]

Here and in many other instances we notice that the Quran not only praises those who are truthful and speak the truth, but it also commands every human being to speak the truth, as well as take the side of those who do so no matter the circumstances.

The invaluable importance of this great virtue is also often emphasised in the hadith of Prophet Muhammad. In one occasion, for example, the Prophet said:

> You must be truthful, for truthfulness leads to righteousness and righteousness leads to Paradise. A man will keep speaking the truth and striving to speak the truth until he will be recorded with God as a *siddiq* (speaker of the truth). Beware of telling lies, for lying leads to immorality and immorality leads to Hellfire. A man will keep telling lies and striving to tell lies until he is recorded with God as a liar.[c]

---

[a] Quran 9: 119.
[b] Quran 33:70.
[c] Hadith in *Sahih Muslim*.

Since lying is a grave evil, from an Islamic perspective a liar is a hypocrite, and the hypocrites are the worst of people. In another instance, Prophet Muhammad made it clear to his community what the consequences of untruthfulness, dishonesty and lying are, and also what awaits for those who avoid such vices: "Guarantee for me six things and I will guarantee Paradise for you: tell the truth when you speak, fulfill your promises, be faithful when you are trusted, safeguard your private parts, lower your gaze, and withhold your hands (from harming others)."[a]

The caliphs, like the rest of their companions, were greatly concerned with this matter, and the following are a few gems from their vast ocean of wisdom.

The greatest truth is honesty, and the greatest falsehood is dishonesty.[67]
– **Abu Bakr as-Siddiq** ﷺ

Truth is a trust, [whereas] falsehood is treason.[68] – **Abu Bakr as-Siddiq** ﷺ

He who indulges in falsehood will find the paths of paradise shut to him.[69]
– **Abu Bakr as-Siddiq** ﷺ

I will not abandon anything God's Messenger did, except that I will also do it; for I fear that if I were to leave any of his commands and ways I would deviate.[70]
– **Abu Bakr as-Siddiq** ﷺ

Youth is not restored by the dyeing of your hair.[71]

---

[a] Hadith collected by Ibn Khuzaymah.

– **Abu Bakr as-Siddiq** ﷺ

Prefer for the people what you prefer for yourself. Which you do not wish for yourself, do not impose on others.[72]
– **Umar bin al-Khattab** ﷺ

Do not be misled by a person's prayers and fasting; look to his sincerity and wisdom.[73]
– **Umar bin al-Khattab** ﷺ

The effectiveness of a prayer depends not on the words but on the sincerity of intention.[74]
– **Umar bin al-Khattab** ﷺ

Good intentions are the most beautiful of secrets.[75]
– **Ali ibn Abi Talib** ﷺ

Whoever does three things with regards to people, they will necessitate three things for him: whenever he speaks to them he is truthful; whenever they entrust him with something, he does not betray them; and whenever he promises them something, he fulfills it. If he does this, their hearts will love him, their tongues will praise him, and they will come to his aid.[76]
– **Ali ibn Abi Talib** ﷺ

There are three signs for the one who works to be shown by people: Inactivity when alone and activity before people, love for estimation and abhorrence to criticism.[77]
– **Ali ibn Abi Talib** ﷺ

A person's worth depends on the nobility of his aspirations.[78]
– **Ali ibn Abi Talib** ﷺ

On Wrongdoing and Sin

From an Islamic point of view, sin is a conscious act that violates a commandment of the Creator or the right of another fellow being. Such sins include associating and/or worshipping creatures of God in partnership with God, murder, adultery, bearing false witness, cheating, arrogance, harming others, and so on.

However, according to this tradition, human beings are *not* created inherently sinful. In fact both the Quran and the hadith clearly state that every human being is born in a state of purity[a] and fully cognisant of the oneness of God.[b] It is later in life that such a pure state is often altered because of various external factors, including family and societal influences. Be that as it may, humans are also seen as equally capable of both good and evil, and this is where wrongdoing and sin come in. On this note, the Quran, like the previous scriptures refers to

---

[a] Quran, 30:30. See also hadith in *Sahih Muslim*, book 33, hadith 6423.
[b] The concept of the oneness of God in Islam is known as *tawhid*. As an indication of monotheism, *tawhid* is Islam's most fundamental concept holding that God is One and Unique.

the "fall" of Adam 🕮 and Eve 🕮 but it does not conclude from it the doctrine of original sin (as is the case in the Christian faith stating that God did not actually forgive Adam's sin and as a result all the children of Adam would bear that sin until the End of Times).[a]

In the Quranic version of the story, after their sinful act, Adam and Eve admitted their mistake and asked for God's forgiveness.[b] And He answered their cry and gave them "a mortal life on earth but added, *'from it [earth] you will be taken out at last.'*[c] Since Allah forgave the sins of the first pair, Muslims believe, all [human beings] are born in *Al-Fitra,* a natural state of [purity and] submission to Allah."[79] Therefore, according to the teachings of Islam, sincere repentance from sin returns a person to this original state of purity. Such a door of repentance is always open to everyone, and no intercession is required or accepted.[d]

Moreover, with a rhetorical question, the Divine communicates through the Quran that people cannot blame anyone for their own doing but themselves because everything they need to orient themselves is already given to them by God Himself: *"Have We not given him [(humankind)] two eyes, and a tongue, and a pair of lips, and shown him the two highways [of*

---

[a] i.e. the Islamic view of the fall of Adam and Eve does not put the blame on Adam or Eve alone, but instead it points out that they both slipped, and both of them acknowledged their error and then asked for forgiveness.

[b] See Quran 7:23.

[c] Quran 7:25. As Murata and Chittick point out, in "the Islamic perspective, it would be wrong to conclude that Adam and Eve would have been better off if they had not slipped." This is because God measures everything out, so whatever happens, it is for the good of that person, even though they might not realise that. After all, God "created Adam for the earth, not for the Garden" because even before the creation of Adam God said in the Quran (2:30), "I am placing in the earth a vicegerent" (Murata & Chittick, 1994, 143).

[d] Sincere repentance in Islam is to feel remorse for the committed sin, removal of the self from that sin, resolve not to commit such a sin again, and ask only God for forgiveness every time that sin is remembered.

good and evil]?"ª Having said this, according to Islamic theology, no human being is born sinful since everyone is given free will to choose good and evil, and therefore, with this opportunity at their disposal, in the end they are all responsible for their own actions. 'Abd al 'Ati explains,

Man is a free agent endowed with a free will. This is the essence of his humanity and the basis of his responsibility to his Creator. Without man's relative free will life would be meaningless and God's covenant with man would be in vain. Without human free will, God would be defeating His own purpose and man would be completely incapable of bearing any responsibility.[80]

Here, in other words, human beings are taken into account only for the good and the evil *they* do in the world. Moreover, as mentioned earlier, the doctrine of original sin has no basis in Islam because in Islamic theology each "person must bear his/her own burden and be responsible for his/her own actions, because no one can expiate for another's sin."[81] For this reason, through true faith in God *and* doing good deeds, promoting what is praiseworthy and just, can one hope for his/her forgiveness of sins and ultimate salvation. The Prophet once said, Forsake sin, for that is the best emigration; and observe your obligatory duties, for that is the best crusade; and remember God frequently, for there is nothing more pleasing to God than that one should remember Him much"ᵇ The following are a few pieces of advice from the caliphs regarding this matter.

One of the worst sins is a person taking his sin lightly.[82]
– **Abu Bakr as-Siddiq** ﷺ

ª Quran 90:8-10.
ᵇ Hadith in *al-Tabarani.*

It is good to repent from sin, [but] it is better to avoid it.[83]
– **Abu Bakr as-Siddiq** ﷺ

Indeed God forgives major sins, so do not despair. And indeed God punishes for minor sins, so do not be deceived.[84]
– **Abu Bakr as-Siddiq** ﷺ

Avoidance of sin is lighter than the pain of remorse.[85]
– **Umar bin al-Khattab** ﷺ

One who does not keep away from sins cannot reach the level of full submission to God.[86]
– **Umar bin al-Khattab** ﷺ

A backbiter harms three individuals: firstly he harms himself, secondly the person he is addressing, and thirdly the person whom he is backbiting.[87]
– **Uthman bin Affan** ﷺ

A backbiter harms three persons: firstly, himself; secondly, the person whom he is addressing; and thirdly, the person whom he is backbiting.[88]
– **Uthman bin Affan** ﷺ

Fear the sins that you commit in secret because the witness of those sins is the Judge Himself.[89]
– **Ali ibn Abi Talib** ﷺ

A man came to Ali ibn Abi Talib and asked him what he thought of a person who committed a sin and Ali advised that the person must seek God's forgiveness

and repent to Him. The man asked Ali three more times wondering what if the man sinned again, so on the fourth time Ali replied: He must seek God's forgiveness and repent to Him; and not give up until it is Satan who is defeated [overcome].[90]
– **Ali ibn Abi Talib** ﷺ

Sinning is a disease, repentance is its medicine, and abstinence from it a sure cure.[91]
– **Ali ibn Abi Talib r.a**

On Justice and Integrity

The supreme virtue of justice in Islam is unquestionable. The Quran states that *"God commands justice and fair dealing [with all]..."*[a] and calls Muslims to be upright and be *"bearers of witness with justice."*[b] In another instance, God makes it clear that He sent His prophets *"with clear signs and sent down with them the Book and the Measure in order to establish justice among the people..."*[c] Accordingly, Prophet Muhammad is recorded to have said, "The best of people are those who are best in fulfilling [rights]."[d] To illustrate this with an example, he once commanded, "Pay a labourer his wages before his sweat is dried."[e] Such statements and actions of the Prophet are plenty. Like the Prophet, the early Muslims were very concerned with the concept of justice. An example in point, is that of the Egyptian man who came before caliph

---

[a] Quran 16:90.
[b] Quran 5:8.
[c] Quran 57:25.
[d] Hadith in *Ibn Majah*.
[e] Hadith in *Sunan Ibn Majah*.

Umar ibn al-Khattab seeking refuge from oppression. Umar granted his request, and then the Egyptian explained what had befallen him. "The son of the governor of Egypt, Muhammad ibn Amr ibn al-Aas, ran a race with me and I won it. He became so incensed at this that he started lashing me with a whip and shouting, 'I am a nobleman's son! Take that!'" On hearing this, Umar immediately wrote to Amr ibn al-Aas to bring his son to Madinah. When they arrived, Umar summoned the Egyptian, handed him a whip and told him to start lashing Muhammad, the son of Amr ibn al-Aas. When the Egyptian had given the son a good whipping, Umar told him to start whipping the father, because, in the first place, it was the father's power that had made it possible for Muhammad ibn Amr ibn al-Aas to subject the Egyptian to a beating. "I have beaten the one who beat me," said the Egyptian. "Now I need not beat anyone else." If you had beaten him, we would not have stopped you," said Umar. "But if you yourself let him go, that is your choice." Then turning to Amr ibn al-Aas, he asked, "Since when have you been enslaving people who were free when their mothers bore them?"[a] As for the next point, the Prophet, as seen from his biographies, was a man of high moral character and integrity. In one instance he said, "Fulfill the trust for the one who entrusted you, and do not cheat the one who cheated you."[b] The following caliphs clearly embodied such exemplary behaviour.

> In the matter of justice, all should be equal in your eyes.[92]
> – **Abu Bakr as-Siddiq** ﷺ

---

[a] Narration in *Ibn Abdil Hakam (As qtd. in Khan, pp. 271-272, 2005)* b *Hadith in Sahih al-Bukhari.*

[b] Hadith in *Sahih al-Bukhari.*

Do not deceive or be faithless even with your enemy.[93]
– **Abu Bakr as-Siddiq** ☀

Use the same measure for selling which you use for purchasing.[94]
– **Abu Bakr as-Siddiq** ☀

Here are the most difficult deeds, done at the most difficult times: to forgive while angry; to be generous while in need; to exercise self-control while no one watches; to speak truth to people one fears or needs.[95]
– **Ali ibn Abi Talib** ☀

On the Hereafter and Preparing for It

If there is one thing certain about this life, it is that it will one day come to an end, whether the person is ready or not. Prophet Muhammad, for instance, is recorded to have said, "[Angel] Gabriel came to me and said, 'O Muhammad, live as you wish, for you shall eventually die. Love whom you desire, for you shall eventually depart. Do what you please, for you shall pay...'"[a] In fact, for one to be a Muslim, they have to believe in the *Final Hour,* the Day of Accountability, where humanity is resurrected and assessed accordingly by the Creator. Based on people's records in this life, their outcome is determined. Therefore, every person is obligated to prepare for their final journey to the Hereafter, with the hope, of course, of ending up in eternal bliss.

Preparing for such a journey is a life-long process. This process, according to the teachings of Islam include, but are not limited to, reading, understanding and applying the teachings of the Quran; studying the life and exemplifying the

---

[a] Hadith in *Silsilah al-Saheehah.*

beautiful model of Prophet Muhammad, the Companions, and the lives of the other prophets; acquiring beneficial knowledge; staying in the company of pious people; contemplating death and the afterlife; praying for forgiveness, and the like.[96]

When Abu Bakr as-Siddiq was on his deathbed, for instance, he called Umar bin al-Khattab to remind him to always be conscious of God and know that God has deeds to be done for Him in the day which He will not accept if done at night, and He has deeds to be done for Him at night which He will not accept if done during the day. He will not accept extra ... deeds unless you fulfill the obligatory deeds. The scales of those whose scales will be weighty on the Day of Resurrection will only be weighty because they followed the truth in this life and it was weighty to them. And scales in which the truth will be placed tomorrow truly deserve to be heavy. And the scales of those whose scales will be light on the Day of Resurrection will only be light because they followed falsehood in this life and it was a light matter to them. And scales in which falsehood will be placed tomorrow truly deserve to be light...[97] Umar and the early community lived by this advice.

> He who aspires paradise should learn to deal with people with kindness.98
> – **Abu Bakr as-Siddiq** ﷺ

> He who enters the grave without any provisions is as though he wishes to sail the sea without a ship.[99]
> – **Abu Bakr as-Siddiq** ﷺ

> *Upon entering a garden, he saw a pigeon and said:* Fragrant good fortune to you, bird! You eat of the trees, you find shade in the trees, and you fly off with-

out reckoning. Would that Abu Bakr was like you.[100]
– Abu Bakr as-Siddiq ﷺ

Have an earnestness for death so that you may be
given life.[101]
– Abu Bakr as-Siddiq ﷺ

Son of Adam! Know that the angel of death who has
been assigned to you has not ceased to pass you and
move on to others, ever since you have been in this
world. But it is as if he is about to pass someone else
and move on to target you, so be careful and prepare
for him (by correcting your deeds). And do not forget him, for he does not forget you. And know o son
of Adam, if you are heedless about yourself and do
not prepare, no one else will prepare for you. You
must meet God the Mighty and Majestic, so take for
yourself and do not leave it to someone else.[102]
– Uthman bin Affan ﷺ

Try to do only good deeds before death reaches you.[103]
– Uthman bin Affan ﷺ

The world is indeed ephemeral, but the Hereafter is
eternal. Do not let what is ephemeral lead you astray
and keep you away from the eternal. Prefer the eternal to the ephemeral. This world is finite: you will all
return to God; be conscious of Him.[104]
– Uthman bin Affan ﷺ

O people! Fear God and obey Him, for piety is a valu-
able prize. Verily the most intelligent person is he who
takes account of himself and works for what comes af-

ter death, and acquires through the light (guidance) of God a light for the darkness of the grave.[105]
– **Uthman bin Affan** ؓ

Having unfading hope makes one forget the Hereafter, while following one's desires deviates from the truth. This world is retreating and the Hereafter is coming, so be among the sons of the Hereafter, but do not be among the followers of this world; because today there is action without reckoning, whereas tomorrow, there is reckoning without (any more) action.[106]
– **Ali ibn Abi Talib** ؓ

There is no better place for your soul than Paradise. So trade your soul only for Paradise.[107]
– **Ali ibn Abi Talib** ؓ

On Trials, Hope and Self-Improvement

Very often life hits us with challenging tests, and at times, such tests appear too difficult to bear or even survive. It is very easy to get discouraged during times of hardship; many lose hope and others may give up completely during such phases of trial and tribulation. The Quran forewarns about this saying, "Do the people think that they will be left to say, 'We believe' and they will not be tried?"[a] One, obviously, needs to constantly prepare for such experiences before being hit by them.[108]

The point of such tests, of course, is just that: a test of life. What we need to do in situations like this is embrace the trials and put full trust in the decision of the Almighty who in fact sends such tests our way for a reason. As we know, there is no progress or development without effort and hardship, therefore such life difficulties are essential for our own development. When one is faced with such trials, they are to accept them as part of life, embrace them

---

[a] Quran 29:2.

and never lose hope of God's mercy.[109] The reasons behind such trials are almost always unclear to us, but not so for the One who sends them. The truth is that not even a single leaf falls from a tree without a purpose. Such a point was nicely summarised by Yasmin Mogahed who said, "Every person, every experience, every gift, every loss, every pain is sent on your path, for one reason and one reason only: to bring you back to Him."[110]

Islam strongly encourages Muslims to have hope in God, and have a positive outlook on life. Hope however should be balanced as humans need to ground their hope, and the best balance is fear, or more appropriately defined as God- consciousness. Speaking of these two opposing concepts, Ibn al-Qayyim wrote that the heart on its journey towards God, and a righteous life of course, is likened to a bird: "Love is its head, and fear and hope are its two wings. When the head is healthy, then the two wings will fly well. When the head is cut off, the bird will die. When either of two wings is damaged, the bird becomes vulnerable to every hunter and predator."[111] Being able to balance these opposites brings about harmony in a person's life, leading to personal-enrichment and self- improvement.

There is always more to any misfortune.[112]
– **Abu Bakr as-Siddiq** ﷺ

If a caller from heaven announced that all people would enter Paradise together except for one man, I would fear that I am him. And if a caller announced that all people would enter Hellfire together except for one man, I would hope that I am him.[113]
– **Umar bin al-Khattab** ﷺ

O God, I am indeed harsh, so make me gentle; I am

weak, so make me strong, and I am miserly, so make me generous.[114]
– **Umar bin al-Khattab** ﷺ

Fear only God, for to Him you are to be gathered.[115]
– **Uthman bin Affan** ﷺ

In the event of distress, man [usually] depends upon his own plan and relies on people, and when disappointed from all sides, then alone he turns to God.[116]
– **Uthman bin Affan** ﷺ

Resignation to the Will of God is the cure of the disease of the heart.[117]
– **Ali ibn Abi Talib** ﷺ

People, I urge you – and myself – to be pious and obedient. Send good works before you and cherish no false hopes. For hopes will not compensate for it.[118]
– **Ali ibn Abi Talib** ﷺ

A hopeless man sees difficulties in every chance, but a hopeful person sees chances in every difficulty.[119]
– **Ali ibn Abi Talib** ﷺ

The servant of God should not fear except his sins, and should not hope except in his Lord.[120]
– **Ali ibn Abi Talib** ﷺ

How foolish is man, He ruins the present by worrying about the future but weeps in the future by recalling the past.[121]
– **Ali ibn Abi Talib** ﷺ

A wise enemy is better than a foolish friend.[122]
– Ali ibn Abi Talib ﷺ

There is no better trade than doing good deeds; no better benefit than divine guidance; no better dignity than humility: no better honour than knowledge; no better chastity than abstaining from what is sinful; no better character than coming closer to God; no better prayer than performing obligatory religious acts; no better intellect than foresight; no better virtue than solidarity.[123]
– Ali ibn Abi Talib ﷺ

On Matters of Faith

Faith is commonly understood in the Muslim tradition to mean "sincere devotion to God with the heart, to testify this with the tongue, and to act on it with the body."[124] This concept, known as *iman*, is outlined using the following six articles of faith: belief in one God, His angels, the divine books sent to humanity, belief in God's prophets, the Day of Judgment, and belief in His predestination.[125]

Contrary to popular belief of many regarding religion, it is important to be aware here that Islam is not a religion of "blind faith." When reflecting on the Quran and Sunnah, one quickly notes that Islam strongly calls people to use their intellect and logical reasoning.[126] In fact the first word revealed to Prophet Muhammad in the Quran was *iqra*, meaning read, recite, reflect, ponder, etc. Such an invitation encourages Muslims around the world to question, study and develop constantly in every possible aspect of life.

In Islam, faith itself, in which "knowledge, emotion and will are all involved, is manifested not in the form of a doctrine or dogma, but in the form of an ideal value." Moreover, faith here "is the moral ground and basis for action and not a dogmatic assertion of salvation- justification..." and therefore, the wellbeing of people in this life and the next depends on faith that is accompanied by good deeds.[127] Having faith means that one ultimately submits his or her will to the Will of the Creator. From this, we conclude that faith is the starting point that leads a person to a life of submission to God alone, which in turn leads that person to ultimate success in this life and the Hereafter.

The Prophet never took the matters of faith lightly. In one instance he said, "Beware of disputes in matters of religion, for they are liable to undo your good deeds."[a] He also said, "The most beloved of deeds according to God are the continuous ones, even if they are little."[b] The early caliphs adopted the same mindset and approach to such crucial matters.

> He who prays for five times a day is in the protection of God, and he who is protected by God cannot be harmed by anyone.[128]
> – **Abu Bakr as-Siddiq** ﷺ

> He who builds a mosque in the way of God, it is God that will build a house for him in paradise.[129]
> – **Abu Bakr as-Siddiq** ﷺ

> Follow the way of life, which the Prophet has shown you, for verily that is the right path.[130]
> – **Abu Bakr as-Siddiq** ﷺ

> Hold on to your *salah* (prayer) because if you lose

---

[a] Hadith in *ibn Abd al-Barr.*

[b] Agreed upon hadith.

that, you will lose everything else.[131]
– **Umar bin al-Khattab** ؓ

Fasting does not mean keeping away from only food and drink, it also means keeping away from lying, falsehood, inanity and swearing [by God without need].[132]
– **Umar bin al-Khattab** ؓ

I'm not worried about God not accepting my prayers, but I am worried about the way I pray to God.[133]
– **Umar bin al-Khattab** ؓ

Judge by what you find in the book of God. If you cannot find a reference in it, go to the practice of the Prophet. If you cannot find a reference in the two, then judge by the principles displayed by righteous servants of God. If you still cannot find a reference, either make up your mind yourself or stop there. If you ask me, the second is better for you.[134]
– **Umar bin al-Khattab** ؓ

He who makes the Book of God as his guide would remain safe from sin, and he would be counted among the best of people.[135]
– **Uthman bin Affan** ؓ

The best among you is the one who learns the Quran and teaches it.[a]
– **Uthman bin Affan** ؓ

---

[a] Narration in *Sahih al-Bukhari*.

The highest degree of faith is that you always regard yourself in the presence of God.[136]
– **Uthman bin Affan** ﷺ

Your charity will not be accepted until you believe, "I need the reward more than the beggar needs the money."[137]
– **Uthman bin Affan** ﷺ

O people, if I gave you the entire world it would not suffice as the price for your faith.[138]
– **Uthman bin Affan** ﷺ

True Muslims have six types of fear. The first is fear of losing their religion... The second is fear of being disgraced by the records the angels have written of their worldly deeds... The third is the fear of having their good deeds invalidated by the Devil... The fourth is the fear of being captured by the angel of death with no preparation... The fifth is the fear of losing themselves in this world's pleasures and forgetting the Hereafter... The sixth is the fear of pursuing family advantage and forgetting God.[139]
– **Uthman bin Affan** ﷺ

Once God has opened the gates to thanksgiving, He will not close the gates to abundance. When God opens the gate to prayer, He will not close the gates to acceptance of it. And if He throws wide the gates to repentance, He will never close them to forgiveness.[a]
– **Ali ibn Abi Talib** ﷺ

---

[a] Narration in *Sunan ibn Majah*.

Man's destiny is his bodyguard...One who does not realise that whatever befell him was inescapable and that whatever escaped him was beyond his grasp, has not experienced true faith.[a]

– Ali ibn Abi Talib

The gift of Islam is better than any worldly wealth. Commitment to religion is better than any worldly concern. Advice from death is better than any worldly advice.[140]

– Ali ibn Abi Talib

The most sincere of people in their actions and the most knowledgeable of God are those who are strongest in their love and awe for the sanctity of the people of *la ilaha illla Allah*[b].[141]

– Ali ibn Abi Talib

"Eternal blessing is only possible when one dies surrendered."[142]

– Ali ibn Abi Talib

Knowledge is the best of inheritances. Decency is the best of arts. Prayer is the best of investments. Good works are the best of mentors. Good character is the best of friends. Gentleness is the best of assistants. Frugality is the best of possessions. Contemplation of death is the best of protectors.[143]

– Ali ibn Abi Talib

---

[a] Narration in *Sunan Abu Dawud*.

[b] The phrase *"la ilaha il-Allah"* is the first part of the first pillar of Islam meaning "there is no deity worthy of worship except for God." The second part is "and Muhammad is the Messenger of God." A person who voluntarily testifies and believes this statement enters Islam.

On Character
and Manners

The Divine created people with different characteristics, features, colours and languages. However, as is stated in the Quran, they are all equal in His sight, and no one has an advantage over another except in piety and noble conduct.[144] According to the Quran, a person should also treat everyone with the same level of respect, and even cherish them, despite their origins, status, background, gender or race, because it was God Himself who bestowed such unique characteristics upon people, as He reminds:

> O mankind, We have created you of a male and a female, and made you into nations and tribes that you may know one another; verily, the most honourable of you, in the sight of Allah, are the most pious of you."[a]

Prophet Muhammad, of course, is known to have embodied this perfect character often reiterated in the Quran. In fact, he is

---

[a] Quran 49:13.

recorded to have said about himself, "I have been sent to perfect noble character."[145] A Muslim understands here that the mission of Prophet Muhammad, among many other previous prophets, "was to elevate the moral character of the individual and the society at large."[146] Therefore, Muslims are to emulate such a perfect character embodied by these most excellent examples. Moreover, according to Muslim thought, good character is the essence of faith, as the Prophet said, "No deed that will be placed on the scale of deeds [on the Day of Judgment] will be heavier than good character."[a] When asked on the topic of character, he also said, "be faithful when trusted and honest in your speech; and be a good neighbour to others."[b] Additionally he said, "The best of people are those with the most excellent character."[c] Undoubtedly, the closest to the Prophet in character were the first four caliphs discussed here.

> Run away from greatness and greatness will follow you.[147]
> – Abu Bakr as-Siddiq ﷺ

> Good actions are a guard against the blows of adversity.[148]
> – Abu Bakr as-Siddiq ﷺ

> If you expect the blessings of God, be good to His people.[149]
> – Abu Bakr as-Siddiq ﷺ

> He who boasts lowers himself.[150]
> – Abu Bakr as-Siddiq ﷺ

---

[a] Hadith in *Sunan at-Tirmidhi.*
[b] Hadith in *Sunan al-Tabarani.*
[c] Hadith in *Sunan al-Tabarani.*

Piety is the most solid goodness, and the vilest of what is evil is vice.[151]
– **Abu Bakr as-Siddiq** ﷺ

Friends of God are of three kinds. Each kind may be known through three signs. The first kind of friend fears God. These are always modest; they are always aiming to increase their charity; they always see their small sins as large because they see a divine rule as a divine rule. Friends of the second kind hope for the reward of God. They display virtue and beauty in all their acts; they spend bountifully in the way of God; and they do not denigrate anyone. Friends of the third kind are the wise who worship God with love and compassion. They give away what they love most in the way of God; they aim at God's pleasure in all their acts and disregard the reproaches of the ignorant; and they fulfill the commands and observe the prohibitions of God even if their lower selves dislike it.[152]
– **Abu Bakr as-Siddiq** ﷺ

Do not be an arrogant scholar, for scholarship cannot subsist with arrogance.153
– **Umar bin al-Khattab** ﷺ

Do not depend upon the morality of a person until you have seen him behave while in anger.[154]
– **Umar bin al-Khattab** ﷺ

May God bless the man who says less and does more.[155]
– **Umar bin al-Khattab** ﷺ

As water drops make a river, thoughts make character and faith.[156]
– Ali ibn Abi Talib ﷺ

Authority, power or wealth do not change a man. They only reveal him![157]
– Ali ibn Abi Talib ﷺ

Don't feel lonely on the road of righteousness because of the fewness of travelers on it.[158]
– Ali ibn Abi Talib ﷺ

A man's worth depends upon the nobility of his aspirations.[159]
– Ali ibn Abi Talib ﷺ

Lead such a life that when you die the people will mourn for you, and while you are alive they will long for you.[160]
– Ali ibn Abi Talib ﷺ

Hide the good you do, and make known the good done to you.[161]
– Ali ibn Abi Talib ﷺ

On Knowledge

Islam places great value on knowledge. However, if knowledge gained does not translate into action, that knowledge is seen as futile. Prophet Muhammad is known to have applied the knowledge he had in every aspect of his life; so did the caliphs we explore here. It is important to keep in mind that the best source of knowledge for a Muslim is the knowledge found in the Quran, and then that from the Sunnah of Prophet Muhammad. As far as the Quran is concerned, it literally means something to "be read or recited." As the Prophet received this revelation from God through the Archangel Gabriel, he recited it to his followers who "would eagerly learn it and in turn recite it to others."[162] As the Quran was being sent down to the Prophet, and as he was teaching it to his companions, they in turn memorised it and others wrote it down.

According to Muslim thought, the Quran is a book of guidance, not only for Muslims but for all of humanity. It also introduces a shift in human thinking, thus serving as a means for positive transformation for those who study it seriously.

Orientalist and Professor of Arabic, Margoliouth, writes:

It [the Quran] has created an all but new phase of human thought and a fresh type of character. It first transformed a number of heterogeneous desert tribes of the Arabian Peninsula into a nation of heroes, and then proceeded to create the vast politico-religious organisations of the Muhammadan [sic] world which are one of the great forces with which Europe and the East have to reckon today.[163] Unlike other Scriptures, however, the Quran remains exactly the same today as it did from the time it was first revealed to the Prophet. There are no versions or variants – just one Arabic text that has been fully preserved to this day.

As far as the concept of knowledge in Islam is concerned, Prophet Muhammad made the seeking of it obligatory on every able Muslim and contended that the one who seeks knowledge is superior to the one who merely worships. He also said, "Whoever follows a path in the pursuit of knowledge, God will make a path to Paradise easy for him."[a] On the same note, he also warned that "A person who, for the sake of worldly aggrandisement, seeks that knowledge which should be sought with the sole aim of seeking God's good pleasure, will not savour the fragrance of Paradise on the day of Judgment."[b]

Knowledge is the life of the mind.[164]
– **Abu Bakr as-Siddiq** ﷺ

The more knowledge you have, the greater your God- consciousness will be.[165]
– **Abu Bakr as-Siddiq** ﷺ

[a] Hadith in *Sahih al-Bukhari*.
[b] Hadith in *Sunan Abu Dawud*.

Without knowledge action is useless and knowledge without action is futile.[166]
– **Abu Bakr as-Siddiq** ﷺ

When a noble man learns knowledge he becomes humble, [whereas] when an ignoble person gains knowledge he becomes conceited.[167]
– **Abu Bakr as-Siddiq** ﷺ

Sit with those who love God for that enlightens the mind.[168]
– **Umar bin al-Khattab** ﷺ

Acquire knowledge and teach it to the people.[169]
– **Umar bin al-Khattab** ﷺ

Become learned before you become a master.[170]
– **Umar bin al-Khattab** ﷺ

Understand the teachings of the Holy Quran for it is the source of knowledge.[171]
– **Umar bin al-Khattab** ﷺ

That knowledge is of no avail which is not put into practice. There can be no practice without knowledge and any knowledge without putting it to practice is useless. That knowledge is blameworthy which is used solely to acquire wealth.[172]
– **Umar bin al-Khattab** ﷺ

Acquire wisdom from the story of those who have already passed.[173]
– **Umar bin al-Khattab** ﷺ

The most ignorant of men is the one who throws away his own afterlife for the worldly advantage of others.[174]
– **Umar bin al-Khattab** ﷺ

The wisest of people question and govern their lower selves, perform good deeds for the Next World, and make use of God's glory to guard against the darkness of the tomb.[175]
– **Uthman bin Affan** ﷺ

The most complete gift of God is a life based on knowledge.[176]
– **Ali ibn Abi Talib** ﷺ

There is no good in worship devoid of knowledge, nor in knowledge devoid of understanding, nor in inattentive recitation [of the Quran].[177]
– **Ali ibn Abi Talib** ﷺ

O bearers of knowledge! Act according to [your knowledge], since the scholar is the one who acts according to what he has learned and whose knowledge corresponds to his action. There will be groups who possess knowledge that does not go beyond their collar bones. Their action contradicts their knowledge; their inward state contradicts their outward. They sit in circles vying with one another, until a man becomes angry with the one he sits with, and so he sits with someone else, leaving the other behind. Their actions in these assemblies of theirs do not ascend to God Most High.[a]
– **Ali ibn Abi Talib** ﷺ

---

[a] Narration in *Sunan at-Tirmidhi*. As qtd. in Furber, 14, 2003.

The sum total of excellence is knowledge.[178]
– **Ali ibn Abi Talib**

There is no good in reading without contemplating.[179]
– **Ali ibn Abi Talib**

He who knows himself knows God.[180]
– **Ali ibn Abi Talib**

Whoever is aware of how the world works knows what the obstacles are.[181]
– **Ali ibn Abi Talib**

The learned lives although he dies.[182]
– **Ali ibn Abi Talib**

The ignorant should not be ashamed to ask, and the knowledgeable should not be ashamed to say – if he does not know something – 'God knows best.'[183]
– **Ali ibn Abi Talib**

More intellect means less speech.[184]
– **Ali ibn Abi Talib**

On Patience, Gratitude
and Happiness

Patience is one of the greatest virtues for a person to have.[185] The Prophet said, "No one is given a greater gift than patience." He also counseled, "Be abstemious, and you will be the most devout of men. Be content with what you have and you will be the one most thankful to God. Desire for others what you desire for yourself, and you will be a man of faith."[a]

Some of the rewards received and enjoyed by those who remain patient, as the Quran notes, include the blessings of God for that person, His mercy, and their guidance in the path of the Merciful.[b] From an Islamic standpoint, a complementary term to patience is gratitude. The one who is patient is grateful to God and content with what he or she was given or not given in this life. For such people, the Prophet said, "How wonderful is the case of a believer ... if prosperity attends him, he expresses gratitude to God and that is good for him; and if adversity befalls him, he endures it patiently, and that is better for him."[c]

---

[a] Hadith in *Sunan ibn Majah*.
[b] Quran 2:157.
[c] Hadith in *Sahih al-Bukhari*.

Naturally, when one is patient and grateful, that person is on a good path to a happy life, as the Prophet said, "He who remains patient, God will bestow patience upon him, and he who is satisfied with what he has, God will make him self-sufficient."[a] As it can be concluded so far, happiness in Islam is not achieved by gaining wealth or fame, but instead, as Aisha Stacey, a Muslim writer, points out, the "key to being happy in this world and the next is seeking the pleasure of God, and worshipping Him, without associating partners with Him."[186] Although volumes can be and have been written on these subjects alone, the following sayings give us a good idea on how Muslims are to view the concepts in point.

He who avoids complaints invites happiness.[187]
– **Abu Bakr as-Siddiq**

While condoling the death of a person, Abu Bakr said to the bereaved family: "There is no harm in patience, and no benefit in lamentation. Death is easiest to bear than that which precedes it, and more severe than that which comes after it. Remember the death of the Prophet of God, and your sorrow will be lessened."[188]
– **Abu Bakr as-Siddiq**

Patience is half the faith, and confidence is full faith.[189]
– **Abu Bakr as-Siddiq**

A true believer is rewarded in everything, even in affliction.[190]
– **Abu Bakr as-Siddiq**

[a] Hadith in *Sahih al-Bukhari.*

Be patience, for patience is a pillar of faith.[191]
– **Umar bin al-Khattab** ﷺ

If patience and gratitude had been two she camels, it would have mattered little on which I rode.[192]
– **Umar bin al-Khattab** ﷺ

Under all circumstances, a person should be patient, otherwise disgrace would be his lot.[193]
– **Uthman bin Affan** ﷺ

Obedience to God is that one should remain within bounds fixed by God promises made should be fulfilled; one should be satisfied with what he has, and should be patient in respect of what he does not have.[194]
– **Uthman bin Affan** ﷺ

Silence is the best cure of the malady of anger.[195]
– **Uthman bin Affan** ﷺ

Patience to faith is like the head to the rest of the body: if the head is cut off, the body will rot. And one who has no patience, has no faith.[196]
– **Ali ibn Abi Talib** ﷺ

Do not sell your conscience for anything but heaven.[197]
– **Ali ibn Abi Talib** ﷺ

On Pride, Arrogance and Being Humble

Pride, arrogance and boasting are closely related to each other, and all of them together, or even separately, can lead to one's destruction. More than once the Quran states that God does not love the arrogant and boasting ones.[a] The Prophet said about this, "Pride means having no regard for the truth and despising other people,"[b] and in another instance he added, "He who has in his heart the weight of an atom of pride shall not enter Paradise."[c] Regarding this, Imam ad- Dhahabi, in his book Major Sins, lists pride and arrogance, together with conceit, vanity and haughtiness as *major sins*, stating that faith itself is of no avail if arrogance and pride exists in a person.[198] From a Muslim perspective, the worst beings in history "were filled with arrogance and false pride: Satan, Pharaoh, the opponents of the Prophet and many nefarious tyrants since."[199]

Islam, of course, offers solutions for people suffering from these diseases of the heart by reminding them of their

---

[a] Quran 31:18; 57:25.

[b] Hadith in *Tafsir ibn Katheer.*

[c] Hadith in *Sahih Muslim.*

true origins and source, and in turn bringing them to their senses. Namely we all came from Adam, and Adam was created from clay,[a] and clay is the lowest and most insignificant of substances in the eyes of people. The message one gets from this is that, given the fact that we all came from clay, there is no reason for pride or arrogance. There is nothing in our makeup (race, colour, ethnicity, or nationality) that justifies a sense of superiority over another. In a nutshell, none of those superficial characteristics are an indication of one's superiority. Here the Prophet said, "The best of people are those with the most excellent character,"[b] and in another instance he said, "The best of people are those that bring most benefit to the rest of mankind."[c]

> He who boasts lowers himself.[200]
> – **Abu Bakr as-Siddiq** ﷺ

> Do not get elated at any victory, for all such victory is subject to the will of God.[201]
> – **Abu Bakr as-Siddiq** ﷺ

> There is greatness in the fear of God, contentment in faith of God, and honour in humility.[202]
> – **Abu Bakr as-Siddiq** ﷺ

> We are a people whom God gave might and glory to through Islam, so we will never seek glory through anything else.[203]
> – **Umar bin al-Khattab** ﷺ

---

[a] Hadith in *Sahih al-Bukhari* and *Sahih Muslim*.
[b] Hadith in *al-Tabarani*.
[c] Hadith in *Sunan al-Daraqutni*.

God bless the man who makes me a gift of my own shortcomings.[204]

– Umar bin al-Khattab ☙

Suffering disgrace when being obedient is closer to goodness than winning honour through sin.[205]

– Umar bin al-Khattab ☙

Do not be impressed by the twitter of an individual. But one who fulfils his duty and trust, and refrains from [transgressing against] the honour of people is the real man.[206]

– Umar bin al-Khattab ☙

I am surprised at three things:
a) [A] man runs from death while death is inevitable. b) One sees minor faults in others, yet overlooks his own major faults. c) When there is any defect to one's cattle, he tries to cure it, but does not cure his own defects.[207]

– Umar bin al-Khattab ☙

The world is full of pride, so leave it alone lest it entraps you by its guises and teach your pride, which will keep you away from God.[208]

– Uthman bin Affan ☙

How can the son of Adam grow arrogant? His beginning is a drop of fluid, and his end is a corpse. He can neither create his own conditions nor escape extinction.[209]

– Ali ibn Abi Talib ☙

Put aside your pride, set down your arrogance, and remember your grave.[210]
– **Ali ibn Abi Talib**

On Seeking and
Giving Advice

Although nowadays many people do not feel like they need anyone's advice,[211] seeking it is a sign of one's humility and care. Prophet Muhammad is recorded to have said that "religion is *nasihah*," meaning advice or sincerity (usually translated as "sincere advice"). From this it is often concluded that the entire religion is encompassed by this concept of sincerity.[212] *Nasihah*, from a Muslim perspective, generally implies giving, seeking or receiving advice. In fact, Prophet Muhammad said that the rights of a believer over another one are six, one of those being that when a believer asks for advice, the other should give him advice to the best of his or her ability.[213] Giving someone advice means that the giver of the advice attempts to guide the seeker towards that "which corrects their affairs both in this life and the next," writes Hussein Rasool, a Muslim psychologist. This also involves "protecting Muslims from harm, helping them in times of need, providing what is beneficial for them, encouraging them to do good ... and forbidding them from evil ... with kindness and sincerity, and showing mercy towards them." Moreover, giving advice, ac-

cording to the ability of the individual, is a community obliga-
tion in Islam.[214] Naturally, giving advice is seen as a noble act,
and one is rewarded for it, as the Prophet said: "One who
guides to something good has a reward similar to that of its
doer."[a] Beside the Prophet himself, the early caliphs are known
for their appreciation and encouragement for the concept of
nasihah, and their awe-inspiring sayings testify to this.

> When you seek advice, do not withhold any facts
> from the person whose advice you seek.[215]
> – **Abu Bakr as-Siddiq** ﷺ

> When you advise any person you should be guided
> by God- consciousness.[216]
> – **Abu Bakr as-Siddiq** ﷺ

> If anybody seeks your advice, offer right and sincere
> advice.[217]
> – **Abu Bakr as-Siddiq** ﷺ

> He who is not impressed by sound advice lacks faith.[218]
> – **Abu Bakr as-Siddiq** ﷺ

> There is no goodness in people who don't give ad-
> vice, and there is no goodness in people who don't
> like to be advised.[219]
> – **Umar bin al-Khattab** ﷺ

> Do not ask about what has not yet happened until
> it actually happens, for what has happened is
> enough of an occupation to worry about what has

---

[a] Hadith in *Sahih Muslim.*

not happened.[220]
– **Umar bin al-Khattab**

Learn Arabic, for it strengthens the intelligence and increases one's noble conduct.[221]
– **Umar bin al-Khattab**

Let not your speech be given freely except to those who want to hear it and will value it.[222]
– **Umar bin al-Khattab**

Do not consult except people who fear God, and do not accompany the sinner, [lest] you learn his sinfulness.[223]
– **Umar bin al-Khattab**

Do not be fooled by one who recites the Quran. His recitation is but speech – but look to those who act according to it.[224]
– **Umar bin al-Khattab**

Don't forget your own self while preaching to others.[225]
– **Umar bin al-Khattab**

Preserve the sayings of those people who are indifferent to the world. They say only that which God wishes them to say.[226]
– **Umar bin al-Khattab**

It is better to listen to a wise enemy than to seek counsel from a foolish friend.[227]
– **Ali ibn Abi Talib**

On Leadership

Islam calls leadership a trust. This is a trust given by the community to a leader to lead the people, protect them, and treat them justly. According to this point of view, leadership is a sacred position intended to improve people's lives by applying God's commands on earth.[228] Some of the qualities and possessions of a good leader include knowledge and wisdom, God-consciousness, justice and compassion, decisiveness, courage, resoluteness, willingness to consult, eloquence, spirit of self-sacrifice, and patience, among others. Research on this concept universally shows that effective leaders a) lead by example, b) are servant-leaders, c) do not establish things by themselves and instead collaborate with others, d) are good listeners and followers, e) help others become better, and f) are humble and always keep in mind that success ultimately comes from God.[229]

It is important to note that our leaders in positions of power are not the only leaders we have. In fact every person is a leader in one way or another. The Prophet once mentioned, "All of you are shepherds, and each of you will be asked concerning his flock."[a] We all have some degree of authority on earth, and have to be constantly mindful of how we use and express such authority and power. Clearly, however, our leaders, no matter their position, have great responsibilities to their people and ultimately to God. For this the Prophet said, "The ruler who closes his door to the poor and needy will find that in his own greatest time of need, God has closed the gates of heaven to him."[b] The caliphs and most of their predecessors where always mindful of this fact.

> Corruption comes when faith is found only in mosques, wealth with misers, weapons with cowards, and authority with fools.[230]
> – **Abu Bakr as-Siddiq** ﷺ

> Be mindful of God and obey God your Lord until the Day of Resurrection, as if you see Him, and obey the ruler (*imam*) ... Never leave the main Muslim body (*al-jama'ah*).[231]
> – **Umar bin al-Khattab** ﷺ

> In the eyes of God he is the best ruler who has secured prosperity and comfort for his subjects.[232]
> – **Umar bin al-Khattab** ﷺ

> You cannot manage to correct people unless you correct yourself.[233]
> – **Umar bin al-Khattab** ﷺ

The ruler whose intention is good, will have the help

---

[a] Hadith in *Sahih al-Bukhari*.

[b] Hadith in at-Tirmidhi's *Shama'il*.

of God in the administration of his affairs. But he whose intention is bad will come to disgrace.[234]
– **Umar bin al-Khattab**

Every ruler should keep his door open to the people.[235]
– **Umar bin al-Khattab**

Whoever is appointed to manage the affairs of the Muslim Community should not neglect his duty towards others, that is to say that he must carry out his duty even in the face of criticism. But those not in authority should concentrate upon themselves. They may nevertheless offer good advice at the same time to those in a position of authority.[236]
– **Umar bin al-Khattab**

Try to be powerful without violence, and to be gentle without weakness.[237]
– **Umar bin al-Khattab**

By God ... the earth will never be empty of the ones who establish the proofs of God so that His proofs and signs never cease. They are the fewest in number, but the greatest in rank before God.[238]
– **Ali ibn Abi Talib**

Speak to people in a language they can understand.[239]
– **Ali ibn Abi Talib**

On Spouses and the
Rights of Women

Contrary to some popular misconceptions about the status and treatment of women in Islam, this way of life has given the utmost respect and emphasis on the position of women in society.[240] As a point in case, at a time when the women of Arabia were seen as transferable property, the message of Islam challenged the wretched status quo and honoured women by elevating them and protecting them with unprecedented rights. Islam gave women the right to education, to marry someone of their choice, to retain their identity after marriage, to divorce, to work, to own and sell property, to seek protection by the law, to vote, and to participate in civic and political engagement.[241] Such rights for women were unheard of in many countries and states in the West until very recently.[a] [242] The Quran goes on to say that men and women are equal in the sight of God.[b] However, it does "recognise that they are not identical" and that God

---

[a] In the United States, the state of Mississippi, for instance, ratified the 19th Amendment granting women the right to vote in 1984; that is well over 13 centuries after the women of Madinah were granted equal rights with men.

[b] See Quran 49:13; 16:96.

created male and female with unique physiological and psychological attributes and these differences are embraced as vital components to a healthy family and community structure with each individual contributing their own distinctive talents to society.[243] This divine decree of equality and respect for women was greatly honoured by the Prophet Muhammad; his life story as a husband and a father shows just that. In multiple occasions the Prophet is recorded to have said, "The best of you are those who are best to the wives."[a] Every Muslim is commanded to treat their spouse in such a manner.

> No man can have anything better after faith (*iman*) than a woman of righteous character, loving and childbearing. And no man can have anything worse after unbelief (*kufr*) than a sharp-tongued woman of bad character.[244]
> – **Umar bin al-Khattab** ﷺ

> If your spouse is angry, you should be calm. When one is fire, the other should be water.[245]
> – **Umar bin al-Khattab** ﷺ

> Women are not a garment you wear and undress however you like. They are honoured and have their rights.[246]
> – **Umar bin al-Khattab** ﷺ

> The happiest [of man] is he to whom God has given a good wife.[247]
> – **Ali ibn Abi Talib** ﷺ

[a] Hadith in *Ibn Majah*.

On Wealth, Excessiveness and Extravagance

Another name for Islam is "the religion of balance." To illustrate this, the Prophet once passed by Saad, one of his companions, while the latter was pouring water over himself from a large vessel to perform his ablution. 'What is this extravagance, O Saad?' said the Prophet. 'Prophet of God,' said Saad, 'Can there be extravagance even if you are standing on the banks of a river?' 'Yes,' replied the Prophet.[a] In another case he said, "Everyday, two angels visit the servants of God on earth. One of them prays: 'Lord, reward those who spend,' while the other prays, 'Lord, destroy the wealth of those who withhold.'"[b]

As far as excessiveness and extravagance are concerned, a companion of Umar bin al-Khattab narrates that Caliph Umar was given the treasures of the Persian emperor after the conquest of Persia, and a companion asks the caliph, "Are you going to put this [treasure] into the public treasury until you can distribute it?" Umar replied, "No by

---

[a] Hadith in *Musnad Ahmad.* See Khan, 227, 2005.
[b] Hadith in *Sahih al-Bukhari* and *Sahih Muslim.*

God, I will not take this under a roof before I have passed it on." So they put it in the middle of the mosque and spent the night guarding it. In the morning, Umar uncovered the treasure and saw such an amount of gold and silver that it almost shone; so he began to cry. Seeing this, a companion asked why the caliph was crying when this was in fact a day of thanks and of happiness. Umar replied, "Woe to you, this has never been given to a people except that it has cast enmity and hatred amongst them."[248]

If an ignorant person is attracted by the things of this world, that is bad. But if a learned person is thus attracted, it is worse.[249]
– **Abu Bakr as-Siddiq** ﷺ

God loves moderation and hates extravagance and excess.[250]
– **Umar bin al-Khattab** ﷺ

O God, do not give me in excess lest I may be disobedient to You, and do not give me less lest I may forget You.[251]
– **Umar bin al-Khattab** ﷺ

You will not be conscious of the reality of faith until your love for God is dearer than the passion to acquire wealth.[252]
– **Uthman bin Affan** ﷺ

One should not feel happy at the acquisition of wealth, nor should he feel grieved at its loss.[253]
– **Uthman bin Affan** ﷺ

Extravagance amounts to thanklessness to God for His gifts.[254]
– **Uthman bin Affan** 襤

Four things are useless, and they are:
a) Knowledge without practice b) Wealth without expenditure in the way of God c) Piety for the sake of show, prompted by worldliness, and d) Long life with no stock of good deeds.[255]
– **Uthman bin Affan** 襤

Riches without faith are the greatest poverty.[256]
– **Ali ibn Abi Talib** 襤

The wealth of a miser is as useless as a pebble.[257]
– **Ali ibn Abi Talib** 襤

On Giving and Forgiving

So high is the value of giving that charity is one of the core pillars of the Islamic faith. Simply put, if one has the financial means, they cannot be a Muslim unless they give to charity. In addition to this, Muslims are also asked to give voluntarily and help the needy whenever possible.

As for forgiveness, one of the names of God in Islam is the Most Forgiving. Because of this, we see Prophet Muhammad being a prophet of forgiveness and mercy; he even forgave his Makkan enemies, who persecuted, starved and attacked him and his followers for years. After the Prophet and his community were mistreated and expelled from Makkah, and their properties were confiscated, when the Prophet took the city in 630 CE, the Makkans expected revenge and the same bloodshed they had committed against the Muslim community. However, the Prophet is even known to have said, "No mercy will be shown to those who show no mercy, and no forgiveness will be given to those who cannot forgive others."[a] It is also known that

---

[a] Hadith in *Sahih al-Bukhari.*

there are countless rewards for those who forgive.

It is related that one day the Prophet asked people to donate whatever they could in the path of God, and the people present gave whatever they had the means to give. However, "One of the Prophet's Companions Utbah ibn Zayd ibn Haritha, did not ... have anything to give. He arose that night and, weeping before God, prayed to Him: "Lord I have nothing to give to charity. Instead Lord, I forgive whoever has brought me dishonour." In the morning when the Companions had gathered, the Prophet asked them, "where is the one who gave something to charity last night?" When no one arose, the Prophet repeated his question. Still no one answered. Then, when the Prophet had forgave everyone and let them go free. He repeated his question for the third time, Utbah ibn Zayd Haritha arose. "Rejoice," said the Prophet, "for your gift to charity has been accepted."[a]

If an opportunity for charity escapes you, try to catch it. When you catch it, try to give something more, or something better.[258]
– **Abu Bakr as-Siddiq** ﷺ

Forgive people so that God may forgive you.[259]
– **Umar bin al-Khattab** ﷺ

The worst person is the miser. In this world he is deprived of his own wealth, and in the Hereafter he is punished.[260]
– **Ali ibn Abi Talib** ﷺ

[a] Hadith in *al-Bidaya wal Nihaya*. See Khan, p. 100, 2005.

Generosity hides shortcomings.[261]
– **Ali ibn Abi Talib**

Forgiveness is the crown of greatness.[262]
– **Ali ibn Abi Talib**

Don't feel ashamed when giving little for charity; that is because there is always goodness in giving no matter how little.[263]
– **Ali ibn Abi Talib**

Kinship, Friendships and Social Interactions

One of the great blessings of the religion of Islam is its commendable success in establishing a close-knit community with deep bonds of brother - and sisterhood. The *Hajj*, for instance, or even the daily congregational prayers at the mosque testify to this process of community-building. It is a call of Islam that Muslims uphold their ties of kinship and maintain social cohesion. The Quran supports this saying that the "*believers are but brothers.*"[a] It further emphasises this in several verses and warns those who sever such essential ties.[b] Like the prophets of the past, Prophet Muhammad was a man who valued his kinship and friendships, even when some of those individuals rejected his message and went against him. On the importance of this notion, in one instance the Prophet said to his companions, "Shall I tell you something which will raise you up in the eyes of God?" They replied in the affirmative, then he famously added, "Be patient with those who behave foolishly

---

[a] Quran 49:10.

[b] See, for instance, Quran 4:1; 17:26, and 13:25.

towards you; forgive those who wrong you; give unto those who deny you; and strengthen your ties with those who break away from you."[a] In another occasion he said, "Whoever hopes that his wealth increase, and his life extended, should nurture the ties of kinship."[b] Another time he said, "It is not right for anyone to break off ties with his brother for more than three days, with the two meeting and ignoring each other. He who greets the other first is the better of the two."[c]

For any community to be successful, they have to try to avoid any dissention and maintain their unity, and especially with their kin. To illustrate this point, the Prophet said, "Shall I tell you who the evil ones are? ...They are those who spread slander, who sow the seeds of dissension among friends, and who seek to lay blame upon the innocent."[d] And the Quran advises here:

> And hold firmly to the rope of Allah all together and do not become divided. And remember the favour of Allah upon you – when you were enemies and He brought your hearts together and you became, by His favour, brothers.[e]

As for friendships, the Prophet has placed great value in having friends, but has also cautioned people who to befriend when he noted, "A person is likely to follow the faith of his friend, so look whom you befriend."[f] Based on their way of life, and their statements, the caliphs in point clearly

---

[a] Hadith in *al-Tabarani*.

[b] Hadith in *Sunan Abu Dawud*.

[c] Hadith in *Sunan Abu Dawud*.

[d] Hadith in *Musnad Ahmad*.

[e] Quran 3:103.

[f] Hadith in *Abu Dawud* and *at-Tirmidhi*.

understood these concepts and applied them until they left this world.

> God blesses him who helps his brother. Cooperate with one another and do not bare grudges of jealousy.[264]
> – **Abu Bakr as-Siddiq**

> You should not quarrel with your neighbour, for he will remain where he is, but your high handedness will become the talk of the people.[265]
> – **Abu Bakr as-Siddiq**

> Muslims should live like brothers.[266]
> – **Abu Bakr as-Siddiq**

> Solitude is better than the company of evil persons.[267]
> – **Abu Bakr as-Siddiq**

> Assume the best about your brother until what comes to you from him overcomes you [and you have to change your opinion].[268]
> – **Umar bin al-Khattab**

> Take righteous brothers [as friends]; acquire them in plenty, for they are a beautification in prosperity and an aid during calamity.[269]
> – **Umar bin al-Khattab**

> Do not seek help in fulfilling a need you have except from someone who wants success for you in that endeavour.[270]
> – **Umar bin al-Khattab**

Repentance, Personal Growth and Health

Islam has put special importance on repentance, that is the person's sincere resolve to return to God and all that is favoured by Him and to stay away from that which is disliked by Him. According to the teachings of Islam, such an act will always bring the person to his or her primordial state of purity, fitrah.[a] After all, our betterment as human beings should be every person's life goal. In addition to this spiritual purity, Islam also calls on Muslims to stay in good health and make healthy life choices. On this point, the Quran states, "*O mankind, eat from whatever is on earth [that is] lawful and good and do not follow the footsteps of Satan. Indeed, he is to you a clear enemy.*"[b] Here and in many other cases two very important aspects about food consumption are stressed: quantity and quality,[c] as Muslims are ordered to eat only that which is permitted and pure, and to not be excessive in this matter, since excess is something that is encouraged only by

---

[a] See Glossary of Terms.
[b] Qur'an 2:168.
[c] See Qur'an 2:172-173; 5:5.

Satan, a clear enemy to people. In our day and age, overeating has become a major concern, and because of it we see people at high risk for a number of diseases, including obesity, like never before.[271] The early Muslims understood this and never struggled with this issue because clear instructions regarding health were given to them by none other than the Divine through the Quran and the teachings of the Prophet Muhammad. It was because of this that the various sciences, especially in the field of medicine, flourished in the Muslim world and later revolutionized Europe which at the time was experiencing the Dark Ages.[272]

As far as personal growth and self development are concerned, these concepts imply the notion of one's enhancement of potential, and a forward movement "from a given position to a position of greater achievement, opportunity and benefit."[273] Because of this, Islam commands Muslims to improve constantly and be productive members of society no matter the circumstances. Simply put, they are encouraged to be better than they were yesterday.[274]

> O God, You know myself better than I do, and I know myself better than they do. O God, make me better than what they think, and forgive me for what they don't know, and don't take me to task for what they say.[275]
> – **Abu Bakr as-Siddiq** ﷺ

> O God, make the last part of my life the best part of my life, the last of my acts the best of my acts, and the last day of my life the best of my days: the day when I come to You. O God! Make the last thing You grant me Your blessing, and a high position in Paradise.[276]
> – **Abu Bakr as-Siddiq** ﷺ

If you want to control other people, first control yourself.[277]
– **Abu Bakr as-Siddiq** ﷺ

It is a matter of shame that in the morning birds should be awake earlier than you.[278]
– **Abu Bakr as-Siddiq** ﷺ

God helps those who are conscious of Him.[279]
– **Abu Bakr as-Siddiq** ﷺ

Every day, nay every moment, try to do some good deed.[280]
– **Abu Bakr as-Siddiq** ﷺ

Caliph Umar was asked about repentance, and he said:
It is that a man repents from an evil deed, and never does it again ... It is that you repent from the sin and never do it again, or never intend to do it again.[281]
– **Umar bin al-Khattab** ﷺ

Judge yourselves before you are judged. Evaluate yourselves before you are evaluated. And be ready for the greatest investigation, the day of judgment.[282]
– **Umar bin al-Khattab** ﷺ

When you do not know of a thing say so plainly.[283]
– **Umar bin al-Khattab** ﷺ

Do not overeat; that invites disease.[284]
– **Umar bin al-Khattab** ﷺ

Death is teacher enough, true faith is wealth enough, and worship is action enough.[285]
– **Umar bin al-Khattab** ﷺ

Sit with those who constantly repent, for they have the softest hearts.[286]
– **Umar bin al-Khattab** ﷺ

Silence is the best cure of the malady of anger.[287]
– **Umar bin al-Khattab** ﷺ

The wisest man is he who can account for his actions.[288]
– **Umar bin al-Khattab** ﷺ

O God I seek refuge with You not to carry me away suddenly, not to let me go astray, and not to count me among the careless![289]
– **Umar bin al-Khattab** ﷺ

The one I love most is the one who tells me my faults.[290]
– **Umar bin al-Khattab** ﷺ

I have seen all kinds of friends, but I have not found any better friend than watching your tongue. I have seen all kinds of garments, but I have not found any better garment than chastity and abstaining from forbidden things. I have seen all kinds of wealth, but I have not found any better wealth than satisfaction with what you have. I have seen all kinds of favours, but I have not found any better favour than advice. I have seen all kinds of food, but I have not found any better food than patience.[291]
– **Umar bin al-Khattab** ﷺ

Whoever avoids empty talk is granted wisdom... Whoever avoids the love of this world is granted the love of the next world. Whoever avoids bemoaning other people's faults is granted the ability to correct his own faults. Whoever avoids prying into the secrets of God's transcendent attributes is granted a chance of staying clear of doubt.[292]
– **Umar bin al-Khattab** ﷺ

If you do not live what you believe, you will begin to believe what you live.[293]
– **Umar bin al-Khattab** ﷺ

Five things are the signs of the righteous. They keep company with those who work for religion. They govern their desires and guard their tongues. They distinguish between good and bad uses of wealth when others are inclined to forget God and indulge themselves. They live modest lives and avoid devouring the unlawful. They think others are likely to be saved, while they are likely to be lost.[294]
– **Uthman bin Affan** ﷺ

There is no good in the world except for two types of people: someone who sins and then follows up with repentance, and someone who races to do good deeds.[295]
– **Ali ibn Abi Talib** ﷺ

Goodness is not in your wealth and offspring being plentiful; true goodness is when your [good] deeds are plenty and you have great understanding and forbearance, and when you compete to worship your Lord. If you do good you praise

God and thank Him, and if you sin you beg God's forgiveness…[296]
– Ali ibn Abi Talib ﷺ

The servant [of God] should not fear except his sins, and should not hope except in his Lord. The ignorant should not be ashamed to ask, and the knowledge-able should not be ashamed to say – if he does not know something – God knows best.[297]
– Ali ibn Abi Talib ﷺ

Not speaking until asked is better than speaking until silenced.[298]
– Ali ibn Abi Talib ﷺ

Blessed is he whose own faults keep him from seeing the faults of others.[299]
– Ali ibn Abi Talib ﷺ

A Muslim should smile even if his heart is sad.[300]
– Ali ibn Abi Talib ﷺ

Goodness does not consist in having much property and children, but in doing many good deeds, in-creasing your gentle character, and adorning yourself before people with the worship of your Lord. Then, if you do well, glorify God; if you do ill, ask forgiveness of Him…[301]
– Ali ibn Abi Talib ﷺ

There is no goodness in praying without standing in awe of God, in fasting without refraining from idle talk, in reading the Quran without contemplation, in learning without acting accordingly, in wealth without charity, in fellowship without offering help in need, in blessings without gratitude, and in invocation without sincerity.[302]

– Ali ibn Abi Talib ﷺ

Today is the day to do good works. Tomorrow is the day to account for your works. There will be no chance of further action then.[303]

– Ali ibn Abi Talib ﷺ

Speech is like a medicine, a small dose of which cures but an excess of which kills![304]

– Ali ibn Abi Talib ﷺ

On Helping and Treating Others Well

In addition to prayer, fasting, and pilgrimage, Muslims are also commanded to serve God by helping others and contributing positively to society at large. In fact, helping others is a central principle of the Muslim faith. The concept of *zakah*,[a] for instance, is meant to help those in need financially; *sadaqah* (voluntary giving) also serves a similar purpose. However, there is so much more to this aspect than just monetary contributions, and there is a reward for every such act of kindness. The Prophet said in a hadith: Whosoever removes a worldly grief from a believer, God will remove from him one of the griefs of the Day of Judgment. Whosoever alleviates [the lot of] a needy person, God will alleviate [his lot] in this world and the next. Whosoever shields a Muslim, God will shield him in this world and the next. God will aid a slave [of His] so long as the slave aids his brother. Whosoever follows a path to seek knowledge therein, God will make easy for him a

---

[a] See *Glossary of Terms* at the end of this book.

path to Paradise..."[a] On the same note the Prophet said, "The best of people are those that bring most benefit to the rest of mankind."[b] In a beautiful narration it is said that a particular Companion, Abdullah ibn Abbas, was once in a spiritual retreat in the Prophet's mosque in Madinah when a man approached him for help. When Abdullah inquired about his troubles, the man said that he owed someone money but was unable to repay him. "Shall I speak to your creditor on your behalf?" asked Abdullah. When the man approved of this, Abdullah set off at once. The man however called after Abdullah thinking that he had forgotten he was in a state of retreat, and Abdullah replied, "No, I have not forgotten, but I have heard the words of the one who lies buried here" meaning the Prophet who had said, "running to the assistance of one's brother and doing one's utmost to help him is better than remaining twenty years in retreat."[c]

On the treatment of people in general, the Prophet has said, "On the Day of Resurrection, God will save from Hellfire one who has saved his brother from humiliation in this world."[305] In one account, a Companion recalls how a villager, on entering the Prophet's mosque in Madinah, started urinating. People came running to give him a beating, but the Prophet told them to desist, and said that the place, which had been defiled, should be cleaned by pouring water over it, and added, "you have been sent, not to make things difficult for people, but to make things easy."[d] In fact, according to Aisha, when the Prophet was displeased with the way someone had acted or spoken, he would express his disapproval of people who act or speak in such a manner, with-

[a] Hadith in Nawawi's *Forty Hadith*.
[b] Hadith in *Sunan al-Daraqutni*.
[c] Narration in *al-Bayhaqi's Sunan al-Kubra*. See Khan, 306, 2005.
[d] Hadith in *Sahih al-Bukhari*.

out indicating which particular individual he meant.ᵃ It is clear from such examples that helping others and treating people as they deserve to be treated are closely connected to a believer's acts of worship.

He who aspires paradise, should learn to deal with people with kindness.[306]
– **Abu Bakr as-Siddiq** ﷺ

When you offer any charity to a beggar, do it with humility and respect, for what you are offering is an offer to God.[307]
– **Abu Bakr as-Siddiq** ﷺ

Be good to others [for] that will protect you against evil.[308]
– **Abu Bakr as-Siddiq** ﷺ

If you see that one of you has slipped, correct him, pray for him and do not help Satan against him (by insulting him, etc.).[309]
– **Umar bin al-Khattab** ﷺ

The noble side of a favour is to do it without delay."[310]
– **Umar bin al-Khattab** ﷺ

I love the following three things [the most]:
a) to feed the hungry b) to clothe the naked c) to read and teach the Quran.[311]
– **Uthman bin Affan** ﷺ

ᵃ Narration in *Kitab al-Shifa*. Aisha ﷺ was the wife of the Prophet

Hide the good you do, and make known the good done to you.[312]
– **Ali ibn Abi Talib** ﷺ

There are two blessings, and I cannot say which one makes me happier. The first is when someone comes to me for help with the hope that I will provide him with what he wants from me. The second is when God helps that person through me. I prefer helping a Muslim to a world made of gold or silver.[313]
– **Ali ibn Abi Talib** ﷺ

On Peace and Conflict

Contrary to popular belief, mostly in the West, *Islam* has a deep relationship with peace. In fact, the word Islam itself derives from the Arabic root word *silm*, meaning peace.[a] From an Islamic perspective, one achieves peace (internal and external) through their submission to the will of God or *Allah*.[b]

The Quran, in this case, speaks of and refers to peace, mercy and compassion more than anything else. In fact, 113 of its chapters begin with the phrase "In the name of God, the Entirely Merciful, the Most Compassionate," and this shows the importance Islam places on such concepts. Unlike some other scriptures, the Quran and the *hadith* present the world and the universe we are in not as a state of chaos but as a place of balance and harmony where peace is the norm.

The Quran calls humanity first and foremost to peace and peaceful dealings with one another, be they Muslim or

---

[a] Silm is also translated as "submission," "safety" and "wholeness."

[b] Note here that even non-Muslim Arabic speakers refer to God as *Allah*, which clearly goes to show that, despite their theological differences, Muslims worship the same one Deity as Jews and Christians, among others.

not, by finding common ground.[a] Prophet Muhammad, of course, echoed the same message throughout his life. In one instance he said, "God grants to gentleness what He does not grant to violence."[b] Another time he added, "By the Master of my soul (God), you shall not enter Heaven until you believe, you shall not believe until you love one another."[314] When faced with limited choices in times of trial and conflict, the Prophet always sided for peace.[315] Moreover, according to Islamic theology, peace is always the norm and war is a carefully considered exception. Even when found in a defensive war, Muslims are instructed to carefully analyse the outcomes of their actions, and if such outcomes are doubtful they should avoid war altogether in order to bypass unnecessary bloodshed on both sides.[316] Such practices are clearly noticed when reading the biographies of Prophet Muhammad.[317] Regarding his commitment to peace, the Prophet often used to recite the following prayer: O God, you are the original source of Peace; from You is all Peace, and to You returns all Peace. So, make us live with Peace; and let us enter paradise: the House of Peace. Blessed be You, our Lord, to whom belongs all Majesty and Honour![318] Most of the world has yet to learn about the true nature of Prophet Muhammad and his deep commitment to peace as prescribed in the Quran.[319]

> You should not quarrel with your neighbour, for he will remain where he is, but your high handedness will become the talk of the people.[320]
> – **Abu Bakr as-Siddiq** ﷺ

---

[a] See Quran 4:128.

[b] Hadith in *Sunan Abu Dawud*.

Do not quarrel, and do not create differences among yourselves. Hold fast to the rope of God and maintain unity in your ranks.[321]
– **Uthman bin Affan** ﷺ

When Muslims are disunited, they will falter in their faith and become bereft of their inherent strength.[322]
– **Uthman bin Affan** ﷺ

Be like the flower that gives its fragrance to even the hand that crushes it.[323]
– **Ali ibn Abi Talib** ﷺ

Do not belittle anyone, for he may be a saint of God.[324]
– **Ali ibn Abi Talib** ﷺ

A person whose heart is occupied with hatred cannot do good works because no heart is spacious enough to contain two opposite concerns.[325]
– **Ali ibn Abi Talib** ﷺ

Miscellaneous

Think twice about what you speak, when you speak, and to whom you speak![326]
– **Abu Bakr as-Siddiq** ؓ

O fellowship of reciters [of the Quran]! Lift your heads! The path has been laid for you, so advance towards the good, and do not be dependent on people![327]
– **Umar bin al-Khattab** ؓ

Once a task is postponed, it is difficult to move it forward again.[328]
– **Umar bin al-Khattab** ؓ

Nothing hurts a good soul and kind heart more than to live amongst people who can't understand it.[329]
– **Ali ibn Abi Talib** ؓ

People are opposed to what they do not know.[330]

– **Ali ibn Abi Talib** ﷺ

Do not make jokes with fools, for they may break your heart with their poisonous tongues.[331]
– **Ali ibn Abi Talib** ﷺ

Appendices

Appendix A: List of Caliphs and Sultans[a]

Rashidun Caliphs (632 – 661)
Main location: Madinah Abu Bakr as-Siddiq (632 – 634)
Umar bin al-Khattab (634 – 644)
Uthman bin Affan (644 – 656)
Ali ibn Abi Talib (656 – 661)

Umayyad Caliphs (661 – 750)
Main location: Damascus Muawiyah I (661 – 680)
Yazid I (680 – 683) Muawiyah II (683 – 684)
Marwan I (684 – 685)
Abd al-Malik (685 – 705)
Al-Walid I (705 – 715)
Sulayman (715 – 717)
Umar II (717 – 720)
Yazid II (720 – 724)
Hisham (724 – 743)
Al-Walid II (743 – 744)

---

[a] List is incomplete, except for the Ottoman period. Please note that the terms "caliph" and "sultan" are often used interchangeably. Also, the meanings of the words, especially "sultan" has evolved over time.

Yazid III (744)
Ibrahim (744)
Marwan II (744 – 750)

Abbasid Caliphs (750 – 1258)
Main location: Baghdad (present-day Iraq)
As-Saffah (750 – 754)
Al-Mansur (754 – 775)
Al-Mahdi (775 – 785)
Al-Hadi (785 – 786)
Harun al-Rashid (786 – 809)
Al-Amin (809 – 813)
Al-Ma'mun (813 – 833)
Al-Mu'tasim (833 – 842)
Al-Wathiq (842 – 847)
Al-Mutawakkil (847 – 861)
Al-Muntasir (861 – 862)
Al-Musta'in (862 – 866)
Al-Mu'tazz (866 – 869)
Al-Muhtadi (869 – 870)
Al-Mu'tamid (870 – 892)
Al-Mu'tadid (892 – 902)
Al-Muktafi (902 – 908)
Al-Muqtadir (908 – 932)
Al-Qahir (932 – 934)
Ar-Radi (934 – 940)
Al-Muttaqi (940 – 944)
Al-Mustakfi (944 – 946)
Al-Muti (946 – 974)
At-Ta'i (974 – 991)
Al-Qadir (991 – 1031)
Al-Qa'im (1031 – 1075)
Al-Muqtadi (1075 – 1094)
Al-Mustazhir (1094 – 1118)

Al-Mustarshid (1118 – 1135)
Ar-Rashid (1135 – 1136)
Al-Muqtafi (1136 – 1160)
Al-Mustanjid (1160 – 1170)
Al-Mustadi (1170 – 1180)
An-Nasir (1180 – 1225)
Az-Zahir (1225 – 1226)
Al-Mustansir (1226 – 1242)
Al-Musta'sim (1242 – 1258)

Caliphs of Cordoba (929 – 1031)
Main location: Cordoba (present-day Spain)
Abd-ar-Rahman III (929 – 961)
Al-Hakam II (961 – 976)
Hisham II al-Hakam (976 – 1009)
Muhammad II (1009)
Sulayman ibn al-Hakam (1009 – 1010)
Hisham II al-Hakam, *restored* (1010 – 1013)
Sulayman ibn al-Hakam, *restored* (1013 – 1016)
Abd ar-Rahman IV (1021 – 1022)
Abd ar-Rahman V (1022 – 1023)
Muhammad III (1023 – 1024)
Hisham III (1027 – 1031)

Fatimid Caliphs (910 – 1171)
Main location: Mai Mahdia, El-Mansuriya (present-day Tunisia)
Ubayd Allah al-Mahdi Billah (910 – 934)
Muhammad al-Qa'im Bi-Amrillah (934 – 946)
Ismail al-Mansur (946 – 953)
Al-Muizz Lideenillah (953 – 975)
Abu Mansoor Nizar al-Aziz Billah (975 – 996)
Al-Hakim bi-Amr Allah (996 – 1021)
Ali az-Zahir (1021 – 1036)
Ma'ad al-Mustansir Billah (1036 – 1094)

Al-Musta'li (1094 – 1101)
Al-Amir (1101 – 1130)
Al-Hafiz (1130 – 1149)
Al-Zafir (1149 – 1154)
Al-Faiz (1154 – 1160)
Al-Adid (1160 – 1171)

Ayyubid Sultans (1171 – 1260)
Main location: Cairo, Aleppo (present-day Egypt and Syria)
Salah al-Din Ayyub (1174 – 1193)
Al-Aziz Uthman (1193 – 1198)
Al-Mansur Nasir al-Din Muhammad (1198 – 1200)
Al-Adil Sayf al-Din Abu Bakr I (1200 – 1218)
Al-Kamil (1218 – 1238) Al-Adil Sayf al-Din Abu Bakr II
(1238 – 1240)
Al-Salih Ayyub (1240 – 1249)
Al-Mu'azzam Turan-Shah (1249 – 1250)
Al-Ashraf Musa (1250 – 1254)

Caliphs of Cairo (1261 – 1517)
Main location: Cairo (present-day Egypt)
Al-Mustansir II (1261 – 1262)
Al-Hakim I (1262 – 1302)
Al-Mustakfi I (1302 – 1340)
Al-Hakim II (1341 – 1352)
Al-Mu'tadid I (1352 – 1362)
Al-Mutawakkil I (1362 – 1383)
Al-Wathiq II (1383 – 1386)
Al-Mu'tasim (1386 – 1389)
Al-Mutawakkil I, *restored* (1389 – 1406)
Al-Musta'in (1406 – 1414)
Al-Mu'tadid II (1414 – 1441)
Al-Mustakfi II (1441 – 1451)
Al-Qa'im (1451 – 1455)

Al-Mustanjid (1455 – 1479)
Al-Mutawakkil II (1479 – 1497)
Al-Mustamsik (1497 – 1508)
Al-Mutawakkil III (1508 – 1517)

Almohad Caliphs (1145 – 1269)
Main location: Tinmel, Marrakesh, Cordoba, Seville (present-day Morocco and Spain)
Abd al-Mu'min (1145 – 1163)
Abu Yaqub Yusuf I (1163 – 1184)
Abu Yusuf Yaqub al-Mansur (1184 – 1199)
Muhammad an-Nasir (1199 – 1213)
Abu Ya'qub Yusuf II al-Mustansir (1213 – 1224)
Abd al-Wahid I al-Makhlu (1224)
Abdallah al-Adil (1224 – 1227)
Yahya al-Mutasim (1224 – 1229)
Idris I al-Ma'mun (1227 – 1232)
Abd al-Wahid II al Rashid (1232 – 1242)
Ali al-Said (1242 – 1248) Umar al-Murtada (1248 – 1266)
Idris II al-Wathiq (1266 – 1269)

Ottoman Caliphs/Sultans (1299 – 1924)
Main location: Istanbul, Bursa, Sogut, Edirne (present-day Turkey)
Osman I Gazi (1299 – 1326)
Orhan Gazi (1326 – 1360)
Murat I Gazi (1360 – 1389)
Bayezit I (1389 – 1403)
Interregnum (1403 – 1413)
Mehmet I (1413 – 1421)
Murat (1421 – 1451)
Mehmet II (1451 – 1481)
Bayezid II (1481 – 1512)
Selim I (1512 – 1520)

Suleiman the Magnificent (1520 – 1566)
Selim II (1566 – 1574)
Murat III (1574 – 1595)
Mehmet III (1595 – 1603)
Ahmed I (1603 – 1617)
Mustafa I (1617 – 1618)
Osman II (1618 – 1622)
Mustafa I, *restored* (1622 – 1623)
Murat IV (1623 – 1640)
Ibrahim I (1640 – 1648)
Mehmet IV (1648 – 1687)
Suleiman II (1687 – 1691)
Ahmed II (1691 – 1695)
Mustafa II (1695 – 1703)
Ahmed III (1703 – 1730)
Mahmud I (1730 – 1754)
Osman III (1754 – 1757)
Mustafa III (1757 – 1774)
Abdul Hamid I (1774 – 1789)
Selim III (1789 – 1807)
Mustafa IV (1807 – 1808)
Mahmud II (1808 – 1839)
Abdul Mecid I (1839 – 1861)
Abdul Aziz (1861 – 1876)
Murat V (1876)
Abdul Hamid II (1876 – 1909)
Mehmet V Resat (1909 – 1918)
Mehmet VI Vahiddedin, *the last of the Sultan caliphs* (1918 – 1922)
Abdulmecid II, *Caliph only* (1922 – 1924)

Appendices

Appendix B: Timeline of the History of Islam[a]

570	CE The birth of Muhammad in Makkah
610	Prophet Muhammad receives the first revelation of the Quran in the Cave of Hira
622	Hijrah takes place – Prophet Muhammad and his followers flee Quraysh persecutions and migrate to Madinah; the Islamic calendar begins
624	Muslims successfully defeat the Makkans at the Battle of Badr
625	Muslims suffer a setback by Makkans at the Battle of Uhud
627	Muslims defeat the Makkan army at the Battle of the Trench
628	The Treaty of Hudaybiyyah is signed by the Prophet and peace is established in the region between Muslims and non-Muslims

---

[a] Timeline is from *Peace and Conflict Resolution in Islam* by Vehapi.

630	Makkans violate the peace treaty. In return the Prophet goes to capture Makkah but it surrenders voluntarily, and the Makkans are forgiven
632	Prophet Muhammad dies; Abu Bakr is elected his representative (caliph)
633-34	The Wars of Riddah take place in order to unite the tribes who seceded from the confederacy. All tribes of Arabia are united
634	Abu Bakr dies; Umar bin al-Khattab becomes caliph
638	Jerusalem is captured and becomes the third holiest city after Makkah and Madinah
644	Umar bin al-Khattab is assassinated; Uthman bin Affan becomes the caliph
656	Uthman is assassinated and many, but not all, accept Ali ibn Abi Talib as the fourth caliph; two opposing camps of Muslims are formed
657	An effort to arbitrate between the two sides at Siffin fails and Muawiyyah (Ali's opponent) is proclaimed as caliph in Jerusalem
661	Ali is murdered by a Kharajite; Muawiyyah I takes complete control and founds the Umayyad dynasty, moving his capital from Madinah to Damascus
680	He becomes the second Umayyad caliph; Husayn, the grandson of the Prophet, is killed; divisions widen; the Shi'a movement arises
687-705	Caliph Abd al-Malik restores the Umayyad dynasty

691	The Dome of the Rock is completed in Jerusalem
705-17	Muslims take North Africa and establish a kingdom in Spain
749-50	The Abbasids overthrew the Umayyads; for the first time an absolute monarchy is established
756	Spain secedes from the Abbasids becoming a caliphate of its own
762	Baghdad becomes the new capital of the Abbasids
786-808	The reign of Harun al-Rashid; a great cultural renaissance occurs in the empire. Scholarship, arts and sciences are greatly encouraged and flourish
814-15	The Shi'a rebel in Basrah
833-42	The reign of Caliph al-Mutasim; his capital is moved to Samarra
912-61	The reign of Caliph Abd al-Rahman III in the Spanish kingdom of Al-Andalus
969-1027	Cordoba is the center of learning
969	Fatimids gain power in Egypt and attack Palestine, Syria, and Arabia; Cairo is founded
1055	Seljuk Turks take Baghdad
1071	Seljuk troops defeat the Byzantines at the Battle of Manzikurt
1085	Toledo falls to the Christian armies of the Reconquista

1095	Pope Urban II launches the First Crusade
1099	The Crusaders conquer Jerusalem
1171-1250	The Ayyubid dynasty is founded by Salahudin Ayyubi
1187	Salahudin's armies defeat the Crusaders at the Battle of Hattin and retake Jerusalem
1220-1358	The Mongol threat; rule of Golden Horde Mongols and their conversion to Islam
1250	The Mamluks overthrow the Ayyubids and establish rule in Egypt and Syria
1258	Mongols capture Baghdad; the city is ransacked and the caliph is killed; the end of the Abbasid caliphate
1281-1334	Reign of Osman, the founder of the Ottoman Empire
1389	The Ottomans take over the Balkans after their victory at the Battle of Kosova
1453	Sultan Mehmet II "the Conqueror" takes Constantinople(present-day Istanbul), making it the capital of the Empire
1492	The Muslim kingdom of Granada is captured by the monarchs of Castile and Aragon; all Muslims and Jews are sent into exile from Spain
1501	Shah Ismail I establishes the Safavid dynasty in Persia and declares Shi'ism the official religion of the state
1517	The Ottomans take control of Makkah and Madinah

1520-66	Reign of Sultan Suleiman the Magnificent; the Empire reaches its apex
1556	Akbar founds the Mughal dynasty in northern India
1627-58	Shah Jahan rules the Mughal Empire
1774	The Ottomans are defeated by the Russians
1789-1807	Sultan Selim III introduces reforms to westernise the Ottoman Empire
1798-1801	Napoleon Bonaparte occupies Egypt
1805-48	Muhammad Ali begins a campaign of modernisation in Egypt
1808-39	Sultan Mahmud II introduces more reforms to modernise the Ottoman Empire
1839-61	Sultan Abdulhamid introduces more reforms of modernisation in order to halt the fall of the Ottoman Empire
1861-76	Sultan Abdulaziz introduces further reforms for the modernisation of the Ottoman Empire but in so doing, he drives the Empire into bankruptcy
1871-79	Muslim thinkers and reformers like Al-Afghani and Muhammad Abdu call for the revitalisation of Islam
1916-21	The Arab revolt against the Ottoman Empire
1917	The Balfour Declaration[a] is enforced in Palestine

---

[a] The Balfour Declaration was a statement issued publically by the British government during World War I announcing support for the establishment of a "national home for the Jewish people" (not a state) in Palestine. This was an Arab inhabited Ottoman region with a minority Jewish population.

1919-21   The Turkish War of Independence takes place under the lead of Kamal Ataturk

1924   The Turkish National Assembly abolished the Caliphate

1969   The OIC (Organisation of Islamic Cooperation) is established

Glossary of Terms

(ﷺ) The Arabic *sallAllahu alayhi wa sallam,* meaning "peace and blessings of God be upon him," and is used after the name of the Prophet Muhammad.

(عليه السلام) The Arabic *alayhi salaam,* meaning "peace be upon him," and is used after the names of the prophets and the Archangel Jibril (Gabriel) عليه السلام

(رضي الله عنه) The Arabic *radiAllahu anhu,* meaning "may God be pleased with him." It is used after the names of the male Companions of the Prophet.

(رضي الله عنها) The Arabic *radiAllahu anha,* meaning "may God be pleased with her." It is used after the names of the female members of the Prophet Muhammad's family and his female Companions.

BCE Stands for Before the Common Era and has been used in place of BC to denote a Gregorian year.

CE   Stands for Common Era and has been used in place of AD to denote a Gregorian year.

AH   Stands for *Anno Hegirae* and is used to denote the Islamic calendar that starts from the *hijrah* in 623 CE.

Abd   Meaning "servant/slave of" and used in (masculine) Arabic names, usually before one of the names of God, like Abdullah or Abdul-Aziz.

Allah   The Arabic word for God used by Muslim and non- Muslim Arabic speakers alike.

Aman   Security, safety, peace, shelter, protection.

Ansar   Lit. the helpers; the people of Madinah who supported and the *Muhajirun* (Emigrants) when they migrated from Makkah to Madinah.

Caliph   Any successor to Prophet Muhammad as leader of the Muslim community.

Caliphate   Islamic government headed by a caliph.

Fitrah   The pure and original human nature as created by God and with which every human being is born.

Hadith   written narrative reports of Prophet Muhammad's sayings, actions and approvals.

Hajj   The pilgrimage to Makkah in the month of *Dhul-Hijjah* (it is one of the five pillars of Islam).

Hijrah   Meaning emigration; it refers to the journey of the Prophet from Makkah to Madinah, and it also marks the beginning of the Islamic calendar.

Hudaybiyyah A place where a peace treaty was signed between the Prophet and the Quraysh tribe.

Ihsan According to hadith, it is "to worship God as if you see Him for if you do not see Him, He sees you." To do a worthy act excellently.

Ijma Agreeing upon; consensus of the community, particularly the learned ones; the third source of the *shariah*.

Ijtihad Independent analysis or interpretation of Islamic law.

Imam "Leader," prayer leader.

Iman The concept of faith consisting of belief in God, the angels, the books of God, the prophets, predestination, the Prophet Muhammad and the Day of Judgment.

Insaan The Quranic Arabic term for human beings.

Iqra The first revealed word of the Quran meaning to "read or recite."

Islah The Quranic Arabic term to denote mediation or helping people to reconcile, repair relationships.

Islam Submission to the will of God alone.

Jihad Exertion or struggle in the path of God for the greater good.

Jizyah Head tax paid by non-Muslims for living

THE BOOK OF THE GREAT QUOTES

under the protection of the Islamic state. Payment of this tax exempts non-Muslims from military service and other taxes payable by the Muslims.

Kabah The Sacred House of God in Makkah.

Khalifa The Quranic Arabic term for caretaker, vicegerent or representative of the authority of God on earth.

Madinah The shortened form of *Madinah-tun Nabi* – the City of the Prophet Muhammad, formerly known as Yathrib.

Makkah The city of birth of the Prophet Muhammad, the location of the Kabah and Islam's holiest city.

Maroof The Quranic Arabic term for good, truth, justice. Muslims are commanded to enjoin others to *maroof*.

Masjidal-Haram The mosque that houses the Kabah in Makkah.

Muhajirun Lit. emigrants. Those Companions of the Prophet who accepted Islam in Makkah and emigrated to Madinah with the Prophet to join the *Ansar*.

Munkar The Quranic Arabic term for evil and injustice. Muslims are commanded to forbid *munkar*.

Nafs The Quranic Arabic term for the self.

Qalb The Quranic Arabic term for the heart.

Qiyas Analogical deductions by learned people;

the fourth source of the Shariah.

Quraysh   The tribe of the Prophet Muhammad.

Quran   "Recitations," the Word of God revealed to the Prophet Muhammad through the Archangel Gabriel 通

Ruh   The soul, spirit that God blew into Adam 通, the first human created out of clay, and which is present in all human beings.

Sahabah   Companions of Prophet Muhammad, those who met him and accepted his message.

Salam   The Arabic word for "peace."

Salah   Ritual prayer (one of the five pillars of Islam).

Sawm   Fasting during the month of Ramadan (one of the five pillars of Islam).

Shahadah   Profession of faith: "There is no god but Allah and Muhammad is His final messenger" (the first pillar of Islam).

Shariah   Legal tradition, Islamic law or "path"; rules and regulations that govern the day-to-day life of Muslims.

Shi'ite/Shia Meaning "party," one who believes that the authority of Prophet Muhammad is to pass to his descendants.

Shirk   Associating others with God, the only unforgivable sin in Islam if the person dies in such a state.

Sunnah   Traditions (sayings, actions and approvals) of Prophet Muhammad.

Sunni	One who follows the ways and customs of Prophet Muhammad, and believes that the succession of Prophet Muhammad is to pass down to any qualified Muslim through the consensus of the Muslim community.
Taqwa	God-consciousness, God-wariness, Mindfulness of God
Tawhid	The Oneness of God, that He is Unique and He alone is to be worshipped, and that He has or needs no partners (also transliterated as *tawheed*).
Ummah	Community of the faithful, refers to the worldwide Muslim community.
Umrah	The lesser pilgrimage to the Kabah that can be performed at any time of the year.
Zakat	Poor-due, an "alms tax," obligatory for Muslims (one of the five pillars of Islam).

Acknowledgments

First and foremost, I praise and thank the All-Merciful for enabling me to bring forth these great reminders from some of the greatest role models of Muslim history. Secondly, there are numerous incredible people I wish to thank and acknowledge for their tremendous support with this work; that includes my family, friends and mentors. Countless thanks to my wife for her patience with me, and for going over my work. Heartfelt thanks to The Mughal Development Fund for financing most of this project and to Stella Williams for proofreading it. Also, my deep appreciations go to Burhan Fili, Didmar Faja, Abdullah Alkadi, Joel Hayward, and Amber Haque for their invaluable support and friendship. Special thanks to Masud and Salma Ahmad, Mike and Linda Tresemer, Maqsood and Eloisa Chaudhary, Kaan Katircioglu, Rania Ayoub, Judith Jensen, Brian Carter, Dan Latona, Imran Maqbool, Lori and David Sours, Amy Lepon, Ahmed Al-Baloushi, Mohammad Al-Rashdi, Ali and Aziz Govori, Fadil Mourad, and the following families: Brady and Wright, Offenbacher, Bresa, Yavuz, Obaidi, Mirza, Jaffar, Rockholt and Manlulu, Petersen, Gashi, and many more. Finally, I am indebted to the translators of many of the quotes and the authors cited in this book because without their contributions this book would have looked very different.

Bibliography

Primary Sources

al-Jawziyah, Ibn Qayyim. *Patience and Gratitude.* Ta-Ha Publishers, 1997.

Ibn Ishaq, Muhammad. *The Life Of Muhammad.* Trans. by A. Guillaume. Oxford University Press, 2004.

Ibn Katheer, at-Tabari, As-Syooti et al. *Biographies Of The Rightly- Guided Caliphs.* Dar Al-Manarah, 2001.

al-Nawawi, Imam Abu Zakariyya Yahya. *Ettiquette with the Quran* (Trans. M. Furber), Starlatch Press, 2003.

Suyuti, Jalal al-Din. *The History Of The Khalifahs Who Took The Right Way.* 1st ed. Ta-Ha Publishers, 1995.

al-Tabari, Muh ammad Ibn-Garir. *The History Of Al-T abari. VI-XVll* (various translators), State Univ. Of New York Press, 1988.

Other Books

'Abd al 'Ati, Hammudah. *Islam in Focus*. 3rd ed. Amana Publications, 1998.

Al-Jifri, Habib. *The Concept Of Faith In Islam*. 1st ed. MABDA, 2012.

Al-Muratani, Muhammad Mawlud al-Ya'qubi al-Musawi and Hamza Yusuf. *Purification Of The Heart*. 1st ed. Dar Al Taqwa, 2012.

Al-Yaqoubi, Muhammad. *Refuting ISIS*. Sacred Knowledge, 2016.

Arnold, T. W. *The Caliphate*. Oxford University Press, 1924.

Badawi, Jamal A. *Gender Equity In Islam*. American Trust Publications, 1995.

Bahammam, Fahd. *The New Muslim Guide*. Al-Kutub Publishing and Distribution, 2012.

Bashier, Zakaria. *War and Peace in the Life of Prophet Muhammad*. The Islamic Foundation, 2016.

Beekun, Rafik, and Jamal Badawi. *Leadership: An Islamic Perspective*. Amana, 1999.

Emerick, Yahiya. *Muhammad*. Alpha, 2002.

Graham, Mark. *How Islam Created The Modern World*. Amana Publications, 2006.

Hayward, Joel. *Warfare In The Quran*. 1st ed. MABDA, 2012.

Hussain, Feryad A. *Therapy From The Quran and Ahadith*. Darussalam, 2011.

Kennedy, Hugh. Caliphate: *The History of an Idea*. Basic Books, 2016.

The Prophet And The Age Of The Caliphates. Routledge, 2004.

Khan, M. Wahiduddin. *An Islamic Treasury Of Virtues*. Goodword Books, 2005.

The Man Islam Builds. Goodword Books (Booklet) (n.d.).

McAuliffe, Jane Dammen, and Jack Miles. *The Norton Anthology Of World Religions: Islam*. W. W. Norton, 2017.

McAuliffe, Jane. *The Quran*. W. W. Norton, 2017.

Muir, Sir William. *The Caliphate: Its Rise, Decline and Fall*, edited by T H Weir. Edinburgh: John Grant, 1924 (republished 2004, Whitefish, MT: Kessinger Publishing.

Mujahid, Abdul Malik. *Golden Stories of Umar Ibn Al-Khattab*. Darussalam, 2014.

Nadwi, Abul Hasan Ali. *Stories From Islamic History*. UK Islamic Academy, 2005.

Qaasim, 'Abd al-Malik and Imam Jalal Abualrub. *Life Is A Fading Shadow*. Darussalam, 1999.

Rasool, G. Hussein. Islamic Counseling. 1st ed. Routledge, 2016.

Redha, Mohammad. *Othman Ibn Affan*. Dar-Al Kotab Al-Ilmiyah, 1999.

Sallabi, Ali M. *Abu Bakr As-Siddiq*. International Islamic Publishing House, 2013.

   ---*Ali Bin Abi Tâlib* (2 Vol. Set). International Islamic

Publishing House, 2010.

--- *'Umar ibn al-Khattâb* (2 Vol. Set). International Islamic Publishing House, 2007.

--- *'Uthmân ibn 'Affân*. International Islamic Publishing House, 2014.

Siddiqui, Faisal Z. *Sayings Of The Prophet (Saw) And Four Caliphs*. Adam Publishers & Distributors, 2009.

Tahawi, Ahmad ibn Muhammad, and Hamza Yusuf. *The Creed Of Imam Al-Tahawi*. Zaytuna Institute, 2008.

Tahir-ul-Qadri, Muhammad. *Peace, Integration and Human Rights*. Minhaj-Ul-Quran, 2012.

Topbaş, Osman Nuri. *Principles From The Lives Of The Four Rightly-Guided Caliphs*. ERKAM Publications, 2010.

Articles and Online Resources

Ahmad, Syed. "Principles Of Self Development In Islam (Part 1 of 3) - The Religion Of Islam". *Islamreligion.com*, 2013, https://www.islamreligion.com/articles/5305/principles-of-self-development-in-islam-part-1/. Accessed 23 Mar 2018.

Al-Hashimi, Owais. "Alī B. Abī Ṭālib - Sayings Of The Salaf." *Sayings Of The Salaf,* https://www.sayingsofthesalaf.net/name/ali-b-abi-talib/page/4/. Accessed 29 May 2017.

"Ali Bin Abi Talib." *Sunnah.org*, n.d., http://sunnah.org/publication/khulafa_rashideen/caliph4.htm. Accessed 27 May 2018.

Beekun, Rafik. "Leadership and Islam." *The Islamic Workplace,*

9 Sept. 2012, https://theislamicworkplace.com/leadership-and-islam/. Accessed 12 Feb. 2018.

"Caliph." *New World Encyclopedia,* 2017, http://www.new-worldencyclopedia.org/entry/Caliph. Accessed 12 Apr 2018.

"Hadith 7: The Religion Is Naseehah (Sincere Advice)." *40hadithnawawi.com.* N.p., 2014. Accessed 2 Dec 2016.

"History Of Khalifa Uthman Bin Affan - Early Life." *Alim.org,* 2018, http://www.alim.org/library/biography /khalifa/content/KUT/1/3. Accessed 29 Jan 2018.

Husayn, Khalid. "Preparing Ourselves For The Hereafter" Islamtoday. *En.islamtoday.net.* 2003. Accessed 19 Nov 2016.

Malaekah, Mostafa. "Islam Guide: What Is The Purpose Of Life?" *Islam-Guide.com,* 2001, https://www.islam- guide.com/purpose-of-life.htm#s9. Accessed 27 May 2018.

"The Rightly Guided Caliphs: Abu Bakr (Part 1 of 2)." *New Muslims E Learning Site,* 2018, https://www.newmuslims.com/lessons/230/. Accessed 29 Mar 2018.

Qureshi, Imran. *Sayings of Caliphs.* Computer Software. Apple App Store. ImranQureshi.com, 2012. Accessed 25 Oct 2015.

Shoda, Yuichi, Walter Mischel, and Philip K. Peake. "Predicting Adolescent Cognitive And Self-Regulatory Competencies From Preschool Delay Of Gratification: Identifying Diagnostic Conditions." *Developmental Psychology* 26.6 (1990): 978-986.

Stacey, Aisha. "The Psychology Of Self-Control In Islam (Part

1 of 2): Choices and Challenges." The Religion Of Islam, *Islamreligion.com.* N.p., 2014. Accessed 30 Nov 2015.

"Happiness In Islam (Part 3 of 3)." *Islamreligion.com.* http://www.islamreligion.com/articles/4342/happiness-in-islampart-3-of-3/. N.p., 2014. Accessed 30 Nov 2017.
"The Daily Reminder Network". Thedailyreminder.org. N.p., 2017. Accessed 27 Nov 2017.

"The Islamic Concept Of Faith." *Islamweb,* 2012, http://www.islamweb.net/en/article/134445/the-islamic-concept-of-faith. Accessed 27 May 2018.

"Top Islamic Network." *Top Islamic,* 2018, https://www.topislamic.net/. Accessed 27 May 2018.

"Women In Islam." *Facts About The Muslims And The Religion Of Islam,* 2014, https://www.whyislam.org/brochures- online/status-of-women/. Accessed 28 Mar 2018.

Yusuf, Abu Muhammad. "Never Lose Hope In Allah." *Muslimvillage.com,* 2016, https://muslimvillage.com/2016/01/17/30584/never- lose-hope-in-allah/. Accessed 27 May 2017.

Notes

1. Although the Shia claim that it should have been Ali to take such a post from the beginning, it is well know that Ali was far too young at this time to be accepted as a candidate for such a position, among a number of other reasons.
2. See *Abu Bakr As-Siddiq* by Ali M. As-Sallaabee.
3. For more on the history of Prophet *Muhammad*, see Muhammad by Yahiya Emerick.
4. See, for instance, *Caliphate* by Hugh Kennedy, 2016, and *Refuting* ISIS by Muhammad Al-Yaqoubi, 2016.
5. See *The Prophet and the Age of the Caliphates* by Hugh Kennedy.
6. See, for instance, *How Islam Created the Modern World* by Mark Graham.
7. For more, see As-Sallaabee, 29-32, 2013.
8. As-Sallaabee, 41-45, 2013. 9 Muir, 80, 1924.
9. Muir, 80, 1924.
10. See Appendix C in *The Creed of Imam Al-Tahawi* by Hamza Yusuf, 94, 2008.
11. See *The History of the Khalifahs* by as-Suyuti (Trans. A. Clarke), 1995.
12. See Appendix C in *The Creed of Imam Al-Tahawi* by Hamza Yusuf, 95-96.
13. See *Umar ibn al-Khattab* by Ali M. As-Sallaabee.
14. See *Biographies of the Rightly-Guided Caliphs* by Ibn

Katheer, at-Tabari, As- Syooti et al., 2001.

15. See Appendix C in The Creed of Imam Al-Tahawi by Hamza Yusuf, 96-98.

16. See The History of the Khalifahs by as-Suyuti (Trans. A. Clarke), 1995.

17. See Appendix C in The Creed of Imam Al-Tahawi by Hamza Yusuf, 98-100.

18. The Khawarij were a deviant sect in early Islamic history.

19. See Biographies of the Rightly-Guided Caliphs by Ibn Katheer, at-Tabari, As- Syooti et al., 2001.

20. See whyislam.org eds. article. Accessed in 2011.

21. Whyislam.org eds. Accessed in 2011.

22. This saying is cited in a number of sources with different wording. The translation used is found in the Imran-Qureshi.com "Sayings of Abu Bakr" app. Accessed in 2015. Source cited as I.Q. from now on.

23. Cited in multiple sources. As qtd. in topislamic.com. Accessed in 2017. Source cited as T.I.N. from now on.

24. Cited in multiple sources. As qtd. in Faisal Siddiqui, 2009. Source cited as F.S. from now on. This source often misses numbers.

25. Abu Bakr Al-Daynuri's Al-Mujalasah wa Jawahir Al-'Ilm, article 853. As qtd. in sayingsofthesalaf.net. Paraphrased. Accessed in 2016. Source cited as S.S. from now on.

26. I.Q. "Sayings of Ali" app. Accessed in 2016.

27. The full supplication is: "Our Lord, give us in this world [that which is] good and in the Hereafter [that which is] good and protect us from the punishment of the Fire" (Quran, 2:201).

28. Abdullah ibn Umar, reported by al-Bukhari. As cited in https://hadithcommentary.wordpress.com/nawawi/hadith40/. Accessed in 2015.

29. Translation used is found in alim.org. Accessed in 2018. Source cited as A.L. from now on.

30. I.Q. "Sayings of Abu Bakr" app. Accessed in 2015.

31. Ibid.

32. Translation from Osman Nuri Topbaş's Principles From The Lives Of The Four Rightly-Guided Caliphs, 20, 2010. Paraphrased. Source cited as N.T. from now on.

33. Reported by Al-Hakim in Al-Mustadrak, Vol. 1, 61-62. As qtd. In https://abuaminaelias.com/dailyhadithonline/2013/02/23/

umar-on-humility-if-we-seek-honour-from-other-than-islam-we-will-be-humiliated/. Accessed in 2018. Source cited as A.M. from now on.

34. Translation found in greatmuslimquotes.com. Accessed in 2018. Source cited as G.M. from now on.
35. F.S., n.p., 2009.
36. Ibid.
37. A.L. Accessed in 2017.
38. T.I.N. Accessed in 2015.
39. This specific translation is found in Thedailyreminder.org. Accessed in 2015. Source cited as T.D.R. from now on. 040 Translation found in Mohammad Reda's Othman Ibn Affan, 35, 1999. Paraphrased. Source cited as M.R. from now on.
40. Translation found in Mohammad Reda's *Othman Ibn Affan,* 35, 1999. Paraphrased. Source cited as M.R. from now on.
41. I.Q. "Sayings of Ali" app. Accessed in 2015.
42. Ibn Abi Al-Dunya, *Kitab Al-Zuhd,* article 164. As qtd. in S.S. Accessed in 2016.
43. See livingislam.org. Paraphrased. Accessed in 2017.
44. Found in Abu Nu'aym's *Hilyah Al-Awliya,* Vol.1, 40. As qtd. in S.S. Accessed in 2016.
45. As qtd. in yasminmogahed.com, 2011.
46. T.D.R. Accessed in 2015.
47. I.Q. "Sayings of Ali" app. Accessed in 2015.
48. Ibid.
49. T.D.R. Accessed in 2015.
50. Translation found in sunnah.org. Accessed in 2017. Source cited as S.U. from now on.
51. See Aisha Stacey, 2014. For a more detailed account, see also *How Children Succeed* by Paul Tough.
52. Ibid.
53. See Shoda, Yuichi; Mischel, Walter; Peake, Philip, 978–986, 1990.
54. I.Q. "Sayings of Abu Bakr" app. Accessed in 2015.
55. A.L. Accessed in 2015.
56. Narration in Musnad Ahmad. See M. W. Khan, 211-212, 2005.
57. Sallabi, 134, 2007.
58. T.D.R. Paraphrased. Accessed in 2015.
59. Ibid.

60. Ibid. Accessed in 2018.
61. Abu Nu'aym, *Hilyah Al-Awliya,* Vol.1, 40. As qtd. in S.S. Accessed in 2017.
62. I.Q. "Sayings of Ali" app. Accessed in 2015.
63. Ibid.
64. Ibid.
65. N.T.,
66. Yusuf Estes in islamtomorrow.com, 2001.
67. F.S., 43, 2009.
68. I.Q. "Sayings of Abu Bakr" app. Paraphrased. Accessed in 2015.
69. A.L., Accessed in 2018.
70. See *Sahih al-Bukhari,* 2:386 hadith no. 3093. As qtd. in S.S. Accessed in 2017.
71. I.Q. "Sayings of Abu Bakr" app. Accessed in 2015.
72. As qtd. in islamquote.com. Accessed in 2017. Source cited as *A.Q.* from now on.
73. A.L. Accessed in 2017.
74. Ibid. Accessed in 2015. 75 A.Q. Accessed in 2015.
75. A.Q. Accessed in 2015.
76. See Ibn Muflih's *Adaab ash-Shari'a.* As qtd. in islamreligion. com. Accessed in 2015. Source cited as I.R. from now on.
77. Cited in Imam Dhahabi's *Major Sins,* 113, n.d. In http:// www.islamtomorrow.com/books/major_sins/majorSins. pdf. Accessed in 2018.
78. I.Q. "Sayings of Ali" app. Paraphrased. Accessed in 2016.
79. See Religionfacts.com, 2004 for a more detailed discussion.
80. 'Abd al 'Ati, 1998, 52.
81. Ibid., 1998, 17.
82. Abu Bakr Al-Daynuri's *Al-Mujalasah wa Jawahir Al-'Ilm* article 2318. As qtd. in S.S. Accessed in 2017.
83. I.Q. "Sayings of Abu Bakr" app. Paraphrased. Accessed in 2015.
84. T.D.R. Accessed in 2015.
85. F.S., n.p., 2009.
86. N.T., 33-36, 2010. Paraphrased.
87. I.Q. "Sayings of Uthman" app. Accessed in 2015.
88. A.L. Accessed in 2015.
89. T.D.R. Accessed in 2015.
90. See Hunad b. Al-Sari's *Kitab Al-Zuhd,* article 910. As qtd. in S.S. Paraphrased. Accessed in 2016.
91. Ibid.
92. Ibid.

93. Ibid.
94. Ibid. Paraphrased. Accessed in 2015.
95. N.T., 69, 2010.
96. See Husayn, 2003 in http://en.islamtoday.net/ artshow-421-3041.htm. Accessed in 2017.
97. Abu Nu'aym's *Hilyah Al-Awliya,* Vol. 1, 18. As qtd. in S.S. Accessed in 2016.
98. F.S., 43, 2009. 99 T.D.R. Accessed in 2015.
99. T.D.R. Accessed in 2015.
100. Suyuti, 100, 1995.
101. See Ibn Katheer, at-Tabari, As-Syooti et al, 126, 2001. Also qtd. in N.T., 20, 2010.
102. This narration is found is Abu Bakr Al-Daynuri's *Al-Mu-jalasah wa Jawahir Al-'Ilm*, 2: 73-74. Paraphrased. As qtd. in S.S. Accessed in 2016.
103. N.T., 53, 2010. Paraphrased.
104. N.T., 52-53, 2010. Paraphrased.
105. Abu Bakr Al-Daynuri, Al-Mujalasah wa Jawahir Al-'Ilm, 4: 116-117. As qtd. in S.S. Accessed in 2016.
106. G.M. Accessed in 2017.
107. N.T., 69, 2010.
108. See *Don't Be Sad* by Aaidh al-Qarni, for instance.
109. See Abu Muhammad Yusuf, 2016 in https://muslimvillage. com/2016/01/17/30584/never-lose-hope-in- allah/. Accessed in 2017.
110. Yasmin Mogahed is an international Muslim speaker and author. Among other things, she is known for her acclaimed book *Reclaim Your Heart,* 2015.
111. Ibn al-Qayyim in *Madarij As-Salikeen.* See A.M. https:// abuaminaelias.com/dailyhadithonline/2013/04/14/ ibn-al-qayyim-on-hearts-the-heart-of-a-believer-is-like-a-bird-in-its-love-fear- and-hope/. Accessed in 2018. 112 N.T., 20, 2010.
112. N.T., 20, 2010.
113. Narration in *Hiyat al Awliya,* 198. See A.M. in https:// abuaminaelias.com/dailyhadithonline/2014/06/03/ umar-on-hope-if-only-one-man-entered-paradise-i-would-hope-that-i-am-him/. Accessed in 2018.
114. As qtd. in Mujahid's, *Golden Stories of Umar Ibn Al-Khattab,* 91, 2014.
115. I.Q. "Sayings of Uthman" app. Accessed in 2015.

116. Ibid.
117. I.Q. "Sayings of Ali" app. Accessed in 2015.
118. M. W. Khan, 62, 2005.
119. T.D.R. Accessed in 2015.
120. Al-Baihaqi in *Shu'ab Al-Imān,* Vol. 12, 195. See S.S. Paraphrases. Accessed in 2017.
121. T.I.N. Accessed in 2017.
122. A.L. Accessed in 2018.
123. N.T., 69, 2010.
124. As qtd. in al-Jifri's *The Concept of Faith in Islam,* 13, 2012.
125. See al-Jifri's *The Concept of Faith in Islam,* 2012.
126. See "What is the Purpose of Life" by Mostafa Malaekah, 2001.
127. See "The Islamic Concept of Faith" in http://www.islamweb. net/en/article/134445/the-islamic-concept-of- faith, 2012. Accessed in 2018.
128. A.L. Accessed in 2018.
129. I.Q. "Sayings of Abu Bakr" app. Paraphrased. Accessed in 2015. 130 Ibid.
130. Ibid.
131. Quoted in multiple sources, one of them being invitetoislam. com. Accessed in 2017. Source cited as I.I. from now on.
132. Ibn Abi Al-Shaybah in *Al-Musannaf,* articles 8975, 8980, 8981 and 8982. As qtd. in S.S. Accessed in 2016.
133. T.D.R. Accessed in 2014.
134. N. T., 35, 2010.
135. I.Q. "Sayings of Uthman" app. Paraphrased. Accessed in 2015.
136. A.L. Accessed in 2018.
137. T.D.R. Accessed in 2014.
138. I.Q. "Sayings of Uthman" app. Paraphrased. Accessed in 2015.
139. N.T., 52-53, 2010.
140. Ibid., 68, 2010.
141. S.U. Accessed in 2017.
142. N.T., 67, 2010.
143. Ibid., 68-69, 2010.
144. See *New Muslim Guide,* 2012 in http://www.newmus-limguide.com/en/your-moral-character/121. Accessed in 2018. Sources cited as N.M.G. from now on.
145. Hadith in Sunan al-Bayhaqi.
146. See N.M.G., 2012. 147 F.S., n.p. 2009.
147. F.S., n.p. 2009.
148. Ibid.

149. Ibid. 150 A.L. Accessed in 2015.
150. 151 I.Q. "Sayings of Abu Bakr" app. Accessed in 2015.
151. A.L. Accessed in 2015.
152. N.T., 20-21, 2010.
153. T.I.N. Accessed in 2017.
154. A.L. Accessed in 2018.
155. T.I.N. Accessed in 2015.
156. Ibid. Accessed in 2014.
157. Ibid.
158. T.D.R. Accessed in 2014.
159. As qtd. in livingislam.org. Accessed in 2017. Source cited as L.I. from now on.
160. L.I. Accessed in 2017.
161. T.D.R. Accessed in 2014.
162. Abdel Haleem, xv, 2010.
163. J. Margoliouth, Introduction to J. M Rodwell's *The Koran.* As qtd. in Rodwell, 1876, n.p.
164. I.Q. "Sayings of Abu Bakr" app. Accessed in 2015.
165. Ibid. Paraphrased. Accessed in 2015.
166. Ibid.
167. F.S., n.p., 2009.
168. As qtd. in alkauthar.org. Accessed in 2017.
169. F.S., n.p., 2009.
170. I.e. learn while a student because when one is put in a position of leadership they will be prevented from learning because of the numerous preoccupations. Narration in *Fath al-Bari.* As qtd. in Furber, 24, 2003.
171. T.I.N. Accessed in 2015.
172. A.L. Accessed in 2015.
173. T.I.N. Accessed in 2015.
174. N.T., 36, 2010.
175. Ibid., 52-53, 2010.
176. G.I. Accessed in 2017.
177. S.U. Accessed in 2017.
178. T.I.N. Accessed in 2015.
179. Al-Ajurri in *Akhlaq Al-'Ulama'* no. 45. As qtd. in S.S. Accessed in 2017.
180. I.Q. "Sayings of Ali" app. Accessed in 2015.
181. N.T., 66, 2010.
182. T.D.R. Accessed in 2016.
183. S.S. Accessed in 2016.

184. N.T., 66, 2010.
185. See *Patience and Gratitude* by al-Jawziyah, 1995.
186. See full article by Aisha Stacey, 2011. See also *Islam in Focus* by Hammudah 'Abd al 'Ati.
187. A.L. Accessed in 2015.
188. Narration cited in multiple sources. See Ibn Katheer, at-Tabari, As- Syooti et al, 126, 2001.
189. F.S., 43, 2009. See also in quranschool.com.
190. I.Q. "Sayings of Abu Bakr" app. Paraphrased. Accessed in 2015.
191. F.S., n.p., 2009.
192. A.L. Accessed in 2018.
193. T.I.N. Accessed in 2015.
194. A.L. Paraphrased. Accessed in 2015.
195. I.Q. "Sayings of Uthman" app. Paraphrased. Accessed in 2015.
196. Al-Baihaqi's *Shu'ab Al-Iman,* Vol. 12, 195. As qtd. in S.S. Accessed in 2017.
197. I.Q. "Sayings of Ali" app. Accessed in 2015.
198. See Major Sins by Imam ad-Dhahabi in www.islamtomor-row.com/books/major_sins/majorSins.pdf. Accessed in 2018.
199. See *Purification of the Heart* by Hamza Yusuf (Trans.), 2012 in http://data.nur.nu/Kutub/English/Hamza-Yusuf_Purifi-cation-of-the- Heart.pdf. Accessed in 2018. Source cited as H.Y. from now on.
200. A.L. Accessed in 2015.
201. I.Q. "Sayings of Abu Bakr" app. Accessed in 2015.
202. Ibid.
203. Reported by Al-Hakim in *Al-Mustadrak,* Vol. 1, 61-62. See also Al- Albani's *Al-Sahihah,* Vol. 1, 50. As qtd. in S.S. Accessed in 2017.
204. M.W. Khan, 178, 2005.
205. T.D.R. Accessed in 2014.
206. Al-Bayhaqi's *Al-Sunan Al-Kubra,* article 12345. As qtd. in S.S. Accessed in 2016.
207. T.D.R. Accessed in 2014.
208. I.Q. "Sayings of Uthman" app. Paraphrased. Accessed in 2015.
209. N.T., 67, 2010.
210. As qtd. in quranexplorer.com. Accessed in 2016.
211. See Glenn Stok's article "Five Reasons Why People Don't Listen to Advice on https://pairedlife.com/etiquette/why-friends-dont-listen. Accessed in 2018.
212. See "Reflections on Hadith 7," in http://40hadithnawawi.

com/index.php/the-hadiths/hadith-7. Accessed in 2016.
213 See Rasool, 17-18, 2016.

213. See Rasool, 17-18, 2016.
214. Ibid.
215. F.S., 42, 2009.
216. I.Q. "Sayings of Abu Bakr" app. Paraphrased. Accessed in 2015.
217. F.S., 43, 2009.
218. I.Q. "Sayings of Abu Bakr" app. Accessed in 2015.
219. T.D.R. Paraphrased. Accessed in 2015.
220. Abu Dawud's *Kitab Al-Zuhd,* article 89. As qtd. in S.S. Accessed in 2016.
221. Al-Bayhaqi's *Shu'ab Al-Iman* ,Vol. 4, 187. As qtd. in S.S. Accessed in 2016.
222. Abu Dawud's *Kitab Al-Zuhd,* article 89. As qtd. in S.S. Accessed in 2016.
223. Ibid.
224. Al-Khatib's *Iqtida Al-'Ilm Al-'Amal,* no. 109. As qtd. in S.S. Accessed in 2016.
225. F.S., n.p., 2009.
226. A.L. Accessed in 2018.
227. T.D.R. Accessed in 2014.
228. See Rafik Beekun and Jamal Badawi's *Leadership: An Islamic Perspective,* 4, 1999.
229. See Rafik Beekun's research in https://theislamicworkplace. com/leadership-and-islam/. Accessed in 2018.
230. N.T., 18-21, 2010.
231. Ibn Zanjawayh's *Kitab Al-Amwal,* article 30. Paraphrased. As qtd. in S.S. Accessed in 2016.
232. A.L. Accessed in 2017.
233. 233 N.T., 36, 2010 234 A.L. Accessed in 2017.
234. A.L. Accessed in 2017.
235. T.I.N. Accessed in 2017.
236. M.W. Khan, 282, 2005.
237. N.T., 36, 2010
238. S.U. Paraphrased. Accessed in 2017.
239. N.T., 67, 2010.
240. See Badawi's *Gender Equity In Islam,* 1995.
241. See WhyIslam.org eds. on "Women in Islam," 2014.
242. See Tahir-ul-Qadri's *Peace Integration and Human Rights,* 2012.
243. 243 See WhyIslam.org eds. on "Women in Islam," 2014.
244. 244 Al-Hafidh Abul-Qasim Al-Asbahani's *Al-Targhib wa*

Al-Tarhib, article 1528. As qtd. in S.S. Accessed in 2017. 245 T.D.R. Accessed in 2017.
245. T.D.R. Accessed in 2017.
246. I.I. Accessed in 2018.
247. T.I.N. Accessed in 2015.
248. Ibn Al-Mubarak in *Al-Zuhd wa Al-Raqaiq,* Vol. 2, 595-596. As qtd. in S.S. Paraphrased. Accessed in 2017.
249. I.Q. "Sayings of Abu Bakr" app. Accessed in 2015.
250. A.Q. Accessed in 2015.
251. A.L. Accessed in 2015.
252. I.Q. "Sayings of Uthman" app. Paraphrased. Accessed in 2015.
253. A.L. Accessed in 2015.
254. Ibid.
255. T.D.R. Accessed in 2014.
256. T.I.N. Accessed in 2015.
257. I.Q. "Sayings of Ali" app. Accessed in 2015.
258. N.T., 18-21, 2010.
259. A.L. Accessed in 2018.
260. H.Y., 19, 2012.
261. T.I.N. Accessed in 2015.
262. A.L. Accessed in 2015.
263. T.D.R. Accessed in 2014.
264. F.S., 43, 2009.
265. 265 A.L. Accessed in 2015. 266 I.Q. "Sayings of Abu Bakr" app. Accessed in 2015.
266. I.Q. "Sayings of Abu Bakr" app. Accessed in 2015.
267. F.S., 43, 2009. Paraphrased.
268. Abu Dawud's *Kitab Al-Zuhd* article 89. As qtd. in S.S. Accessed in 2017.
269. Ibid.
270. Ibid.
271. The quality of the food consumed, of course, among other factors, has also contributed to the issue of obesity. See Hussain's *Therapy from the Quran and Ahadith,* 161-166.
272. See Mark Graham's *How Islam Created the Modern World,* 2006, among others.
273. Syed I. Ahmad. As qtd. in I.R. Accessed in 2015.
274. See *The Productive Muslim by Muhammad Faris,* 2016.
275. Suyuti, 100, 1995.
276. N.T. 18-21, 2010.
277. F.S., 43, 2009.

278. I.Q. "Sayings of Abu Bakr" app. Paraphrased. Accessed in 2015.
279. Ibid. Paraphrased.
280. Ibid.
281. Al-Tabari in *Tafsir Al-Tabari* in the commentary on Surah Al-Tahrim. Paraphrased. As qtd. in S.S. Accessed in 2016.
282. T.D.R. Accessed in 2014.
283. A.L. Accessed in 2018.
284. A.L. Accessed in 2018.
285. T.D.R. Accessed in 2014.
286. Ibid. Accessed in 2016.
287. A.L. Accessed in 2015.
288. F.S., n.p., 2009.
289. N.T., 37, 2010
290. N.T. 33-36, 2010.
291. Ibid. 292 Ibid.
292. Ibid.
293. Ibid. 294 Ibid., 52-53, 2010.
294. Ibid., 52-53, 2010.
295. S.U. Accessed in 2017.
296. Ibn 'Asakir in *Al-Tawbah* article 13. As qtd. in S.S. Paraphrased. Accessed in 2017.
297. Al-Baihaqi in *Shu'ab Al-Îmân*, Vol. 12, 195. As qtd. in S.S. Paraphrased. Accessed in 2017.
298. N.T., 66, 2010.
299. As qtd. in islamic-quotes.com. Accessed in 2017.
300. N.T., 67, 2010.
301. S.U. Accessed in 2017. 302 N.T., 66, 2010.
302. N.T., 66, 2010.
303. Ibid.
304. T.D.R. Accessed in 2015.
305. M.W. Khan, 112, 2005.
306. F.S., 43, 2009.
307. A.L. Paraphrased. Accessed in 2015.
308. I.Q. "Sayings of Abu Bakr" app. Accessed in 2015.
309. T.D.R. Accessed in 2015.
310. N.T., 36, 2010.
311. I.Q. "Sayings of Uthman" app. Accessed in 2015.
312. T.D.R. Accessed in 2017.
313. N.T., 58-59, 2010.
314. *Jami Bayan al-Ilm.* See M.W. Khan, 210, 2005.

315. See *War and Peace in the Life of Prophet Muhammad* by Zakaria Bashier, 2016.
316. See Joel Hayward's *Warfare in the Quran*, 2012.
317. See, for instance, *Muhammad* by Yahiya Emerick, *Peace and Conflict Resolution in Islam* by Flamur Vehapi, and *Warfare in the Quran* by Joel Hayward.
318. See M.W.Khan, 36-37 in *The Man Islam Builds* (n.d).
319. See Joel Hayward's *Warfare in the Quran*, 2012.
320. 320 A.L. Accessed in 2015. 321 T.I.N. Accessed in 2015.
321. T.I.N. Accessed in 2015.
322. I.Q. "Sayings of Uthman" app. Paraphrased. Accessed in 2015.
323. T.D.R. Accessed in 2014.
324. See H.Y., 2012.
325. N.T., 67, 2010.
326. Ibid., 19, 2010.
327. Quoted by Imam al-Nawawi in Furber, 26, 2003.
328. Ibid., 36, 2010.
329. T.D.R. Accessed in 2014.
330. N.T., 66, 2010.
331. Ibid., 67, 2010.